# THE ELBE CYCLE ROUTE

# THE ELBE CYCLE ROUTE

### ELBERADWEG
### CZECHIA AND GERMANY TO THE NORTH SEA

by Mike Wells

JUNIPER HOUSE, MURLEY MOSS,
OXENHOLME ROAD, KENDAL, CUMBRIA LA9 7RL
www.cicerone.co.uk

© Mike Wells 2022
First edition 2022
ISBN: 978 1 78631 055 2

Printed by Severn, Gloucester, on responsibly sourced paper
A catalogue record for this book is available from the British Library.

Route mapping by Lovell Johns www.lovelljohns.com
All photographs are by the author unless otherwise stated.
Contains OpenStreetMap.org data © OpenStreetMap
contributors, CC-BY-SA. NASA relief data courtesy of ESRI

## Updates to this guide

While every effort is made by our authors to ensure the accuracy of guidebooks as they go to print, changes can occur during the lifetime of an edition. This guidebook was researched, written and finalised before the COVID-19 pandemic. While we are not aware of any significant changes to routes or facilities at the time of printing, it is likely that the current situation will give rise to more changes than would usually be expected. Any updates that we know of for this guide will be on the Cicerone website (www.cicerone.co.uk/1055/updates), so please check before planning your trip. We also advise that you check information about such things as transport, accommodation and shops locally.

We are always grateful for information about any discrepancies between a guidebook and the facts on the ground, sent by email to updates@cicerone.co.uk or by post to Cicerone, Juniper House, Murley Moss, Oxenholme Road, Kendal, LA9 7RL.

**Register your book:** To sign up to receive free updates, special offers and GPX files where available, register your book at www.cicerone.co.uk.

## Note on mapping

The route maps in this guide are derived from publicly available data, databases and crowd-sourced data. As such they have not been through the detailed checking procedures that would generally be applied to a published map from an official mapping agency. However, we have reviewed them closely in the light of local knowledge as part of the preparation of this guide.

*Front cover:* The old harbour in Stade (Stage 27)

# CONTENTS

### Dedication

*This book is dedicated to Christine, my partner of 23 years and companion on the research trips for all my walking and cycling guides. She died a few weeks after we had completed this guide, though she lives on in pictures throughout the book.*

# ROUTE SUMMARY TABLE

| Stage | Start | Finish | Via | Distance (km) | Page |
|-------|-------|--------|-----|---------------|------|
| **Bohemia** | | | | | |
| Prologue | Vrchlabí | Labská bouda | Labe valley | 26.5 | 46 |
| 1 | Labská bouda | Hostinné | mountain route | 40 | 50 |
| 2 | Hostinné | Jaroměř | | 35.5 | 57 |
| 3 | Jaroměř | Pardubice | | 46 | 65 |
| 4 | Pardubice | Kolín | | 52 | 74 |
| 5 | Kolín | Nymburk | | 27.5 | 81 |
| 6 | Nymburk | Libeň (Prague) | Lázně Toušeň | 54.5 | 87 |
| 7 | Libeň (Prague) | Mělník | Vltava valley | 52 | 97 |
| 7A | Lázně Toušeň | Mělník | Labe valley | 33.5 | 105 |
| 8 | Mělník | Litoměřice | | 47 | 110 |
| 9 | Litoměřice | Děčín | | 50.5 | 117 |
| 10 | Děčín | Bad Schandau | | 21 | 124 |
| **Saxony and Saxony-Anhalt** | | | | | |
| 11 | Bad Schandau | Dresden | | 46 | 128 |
| 12 | Dresden | Meissen | | 25.5 | 137 |
| 13 | Meissen | Riesa | | 25.5 | 142 |
| 14 | Riesa | Torgau | | 50 | 147 |
| 15 | Torgau | Wittenberg | | 68.5 | 154 |
| 16 | Wittenberg | Dessau | | 39 | 163 |
| 17 | Dessau | Barby | | 41.5 | 172 |
| 18 | Barby | Magdeburg | | 36.5 | 177 |
| 19 | Magdeburg | Rogätz | | 31.5 | 185 |
| 20 | Rogätz | Tangermünde | | 40 | 190 |
| 21 | Tangermünde | Havelberg | | 36.5 | 195 |
| 22 | Havelberg | Wittenberge | | 37 | 201 |
| 23 | Wittenberge | Dömitz | | 53 | 206 |
| **Lower Saxony** | | | | | |
| 24 | Dömitz | Bleckede | | 53.5 | 211 |
| 25 | Bleckede | Geesthacht | | 40 | 218 |
| 26 | Geesthacht | Hamburg | | 39.5 | 225 |
| 27 | Hamburg | Stade | | 42 (+3 ferry) | 232 |
| 28 | Stade | Freiburg | | 41.5 | 239 |
| 29 | Freiburg | Cuxhaven | | 51.5 | 244 |

**Total distance   1227**

## Suggested schedules

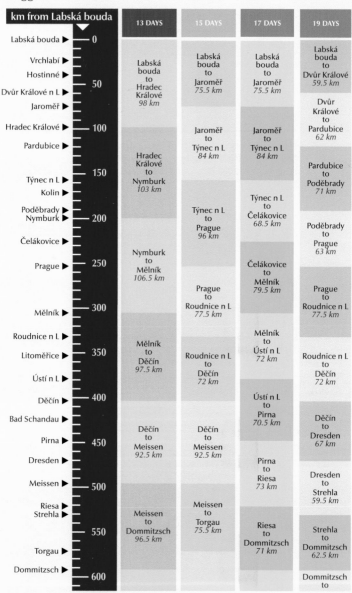

| km from Labská bouda | 13 DAYS | 15 DAYS | 17 DAYS | 19 DAYS |
|---|---|---|---|---|
| Labská bouda ▶ — 0 | | | | |
| Vrchlabí ▶ | Labská bouda to Hradec Králové *98 km* | Labská bouda to Jaroměř *75.5 km* | Labská bouda to Jaroměř *75.5 km* | Labská bouda to Dvůr Králové *59.5 km* |
| Hostinné ▶ | | | | |
| Dvůr Králové n L ▶ — 50 | | | | |
| Jaroměř ▶ | | | | Dvůr Králové to Pardubice *62 km* |
| Hradec Králové ▶ — 100 | | Jaroměř to Týnec n L *84 km* | Jaroměř to Týnec n L *84 km* | |
| Pardubice ▶ | Hradec Králové to Nymburk *103 km* | | | Pardubice to Poděbrady *71 km* |
| Týnec n L ▶ — 150 | | Týnec n L to Prague *96 km* | Týnec n L to Čelákovice *68.5 km* | |
| Kolin ▶ | | | | |
| Poděbrady ▶ | | | | Poděbrady to Prague *63 km* |
| Nymburk ▶ — 200 | | | | |
| Čelákovice ▶ | Nymburk to Mělník *106.5 km* | | Čelákovice to Mělník *79.5 km* | |
| Prague ▶ — 250 | | Prague to Roudnice n L *77.5 km* | | Prague to Roudnice n L *77.5 km* |
| Mělník ▶ — 300 | | | Mělník to Ústí n L *72 km* | |
| Roudnice n L ▶ | Mělník to Děčín *97.5 km* | Roudnice n L to Děčín *72 km* | | Roudnice n L to Děčín *72 km* |
| Litoměřice ▶ — 350 | | | | |
| Ústí n L ▶ | | | Ústí n L to Pirna *70.5 km* | |
| Děčín ▶ — 400 | | | | Děčín to Dresden *67 km* |
| Bad Schandau ▶ | Děčín to Meissen *92.5 km* | Děčín to Meissen *92.5 km* | | |
| Pirna ▶ — 450 | | | Pirna to Riesa *73 km* | |
| Dresden ▶ | | | | Dresden to Strehla *59.5 km* |
| Meissen ▶ — 500 | | | | |
| Riesa ▶ | Meissen to Dommitzsch *96.5 km* | Meissen to Torgau *75.5 km* | Riesa to Dommitzsch *71 km* | Strehla to Dommitzsch *62.5 km* |
| Strehla ▶ | | | | |
| — 550 | | | | |
| Torgau ▶ | | | | Dommitzsch to |
| Dommitzsch ▶ — 600 | | | | |

## km from Labskà bouda

| Distance marker | Cities |
|---|---|
| 650 | Wittenberg ▶, Wörlitz ▶, Dessau ▶ |
| 700 | Aken ▶ |
| 750 | Schönebeck ▶, Magdeburg ▶ |
| 800 | Bertingen ▶ |
| 850 | Tangermünde ▶, Havelberg ▶ |
| 900 | Wittenberge ▶ |
| 950 | Dömitz ▶, Hitzacker ▶ |
| 1000 | Bleckede ▶ |
| 1050 | Lauenburg ▶, Geesthacht ▶ |
| 1100 | Hamburg ▶ |
| 1150 | Stade ▶, Wischhafen ▶, Freiburg ▶ |
| 1200 | Cuxhaven ▶ |

| 13 DAYS | 15 DAYS | 17 DAYS | 19 DAYS |
|---|---|---|---|
| Dommitzsch to Aken 104 km | Dommitzsch to Wörlitz 90 km | Dommitzsch to Wörlitz 69 km | Wittenberg 47.5 km |
| | | | Wittenberg to Aken 56.5 km |
| Aken to Bertingen 100.5 km | Wörlitz to Schönebeck 79 km | Wörlitz to Schönebeck 79 km | Aken to Magdeburg 60.5 km |
| | Schönebeck to Tangermünde 88 km | Schönebeck to Tangermünde 88 km | Magdeburg to Tangermünde 71.5 km |
| Bertingen to Wittenberge 105 km | Tangermünde to Wittenberge 73.5 km | Tangermünde to Wittenberge 73.5 km | Tangermünde to Wittenberge 73.5 km |
| Wittenberge to Bleckede 106.5 km | Wittenberge to Hitzacker 74.5 km | Wittenberge to Hitzacker 74.5 km | Wittenberge to Hitzacker 74.5 km |
| | Hitzacker to Geesthacht 72 km | Hitzacker to Lauenburg 55 km | Hitzacker to Lauenburg 55 km |
| Bleckede to Hamburg 79.5 km | | Lauenburg to Hamburg 56.5 km | Lauenburg to Hamburg 56.5 km |
| | Geesthacht to Stade 84.5 km | | |
| Hamburg to Freiburg 86.5 km | | Hamburg to Wischhafen 78.5 km | Hamburg to Wischhafen 78.5 km |
| Freiburg to Cuxhaven 51.5 km | Stade to Cuxhaven 93 km | Wischhafen to Cuxhaven 59.5 km | Wischhafen to Cuxhaven 59.5 km |

*Magdeburg cathedral took over 300 years to build (Stage 18)*

# INTRODUCTION

*Cycling along the Elbe flood dyke towards Tangermünde (Stage 20)*

The 1094km-long Elbe is western Europe's third longest river after the Danube and Rhine. A waymarked cycle route follows the river from a kilometre below its source in the Krkonoše mountains of northern Czechia (the official short name for the Czech Republic) through former East Germany all the way to its mouth at Cuxhaven on the North Sea coast of western Germany. This route is mostly asphalt surfaced, either on dedicated cycle tracks or quiet country roads, though there are some stretches on gravel or unsurfaced tracks. After descending 40km from the mountains, the track continues gently downhill all the way to the sea, making it the easiest long-distance cycle route in Europe as far as gradients are concerned.

Before 1990, it was impossible to cycle the length of the river. When the Second World War ended in 1945, Soviet Russian troops had control of eastern Europe, including Czechoslovakia and East Germany. Russian political power was exerted over these countries, which became Soviet satellite nations. A heavily armed border, dubbed by Winston Churchill as an 'Iron Curtain', was constructed by the Soviets to divide eastern and western Europe. Most of the Elbe fell to the east of this border, and only the last 300km through the former West German *länder* (regions) of Lower Saxony and Hamburg was open to free travel. When the Soviet system collapsed in 1989, the border between East and West Germany was abolished, while that between Czechoslovakia and East Germany became first an easily crossed border before being abolished in 2004 when Czechia joined the European Union. As a result, free movement became possible along the whole length of the river.

There is plenty to see and visit on the Elbe cycleway, including three great cities, plus another just off the river. Dresden, the former capital of Saxony, is a city that was all but destroyed by bombing in 1945, then suffered 45 years of neglect under Communism. Since 1990, the city has been reborn. Palaces, cathedrals, churches and other Baroque and Rococo buildings have been restored, while many concrete Communist-era buildings have been demolished and replaced with more attractive structures. Further north, similar restoration and rebuilding has turned Magdeburg from a dour east European industrial city into an attractive place to visit. Shortly before the river estuary, Germany's second largest city, Hamburg, has seen its old brick warehouse district of Speicherstadt, on a series of islands in the Elbe, renovated in spectacular fashion. Although the river does not pass through the Czech

capital Prague, a short detour into the nearby Vltava valley enables cyclists to visit the city and see its famous castle, bridge and old town.

Of the large towns passed, Pardubice in Czechia is the home of the world's most challenging horse race, while Meissen, north of Dresden, is a leading centre for the production of high-quality European porcelain. Wittenberg was the home of Martin Luther whose protest in 1517 against excesses in the Catholic church led to the Protestant Reformation, while in nearby Dessau you can visit the Bauhaus school that influenced greatly the Modernist architectural movement. Smaller towns suffered under Communism in one of two ways; either they were over-industrialised with large now-derelict factories and tower blocks of workers' flats, or they were ignored and allowed to deteriorate. This latter group includes Litoměřice, Torgau and Tangermünde, all towns with little Communist industrialisation but with intact medieval centres that with care and attention have been brought back to life.

The route passes three great fortresses, built at considerable expense but none of which ever fired a shot in anger. Josefov and Theresienstadt in Czechia were built by the Habsburg rulers of Austro-Hungary to defend their empire against Prussia, while Königstein, on a hilltop in Saxony, was built by the Saxons to defend against the Habsburgs, but later used unsuccessfully for protection from

*The Czech/German border is nowadays an open crossing place (Stage 10)*

Prussian invasion. The greatest scenic attraction lies on the border between Czechia and Germany where the Elbe has cut two great gorges. On the Czech side is the Porta Bohemica, where the romantic ruins of medieval Střekov castle stand on top of an old volcanic cone overlooking the river. Then in Germany, Saxon Switzerland is a forested gorge through the Elbesandsteingebirge range surmounted by fantastic rock formations of weathered sandstone.

A fascinating aspect of the journey is to see how Czechia and East Germany have developed since the end of Communism. Apart from a few post-industrial towns surrounded by derelict factories and the evidence of declining urban populations, much of both countries is now indistinct from their western neighbours. In particular, great parts of the DDR now look and feel like western Germany; not surprising considering the huge amount of money spent by the German government bringing eastern infrastructure up to western standards.

## HISTORICAL BACKGROUND

Following the break-up of Czechoslovakia in 1993, the former Czech regions of Bohemia and Moravia became a country known in English as 'The Czech Republic'. Subsequently there were moves to adopt a more succinct name and in 2016 the Czech government approved 'Czechia' as the official short name for the country. This name is used throughout this guide.

13

## Tribal roots

The Elbe basin is populated by two ethnic groups, Slavs in Czechia and Germans in Germany. Germanic tribes arrived first, moving south from Scandinavia around 200BC, while the Slavs are relative newcomers, arriving from eastern Europe between the sixth and the eighth centuries AD.

At about the same time as the Germans arrived, Czechia was being settled by Celtic tribes pushed out of northern Italy and over the Alps by the Romans, particularly the Boii from which the name Bohemia is derived (*Boii-heimat*, German for Boii homeland). Though they captured southern Germany, an attempt by the Romans to capture the rest of the country was halted by a combined force of Germanic tribes at the Battle of the Teutoberg forest (AD9), described by Tacitus as 'the greatest defeat the Romans ever suffered'. As a result, Roman civilisation never reached the Elbe basin which remained in the hands of many disparate tribes.

## The Great Migrations

These tribal boundaries lasted until AD375, when the Huns (a non-Germanic tribe) arrived in eastern Europe from the Asian steppes, beginning a period known as the 'Great Migrations'. A fiercely aggressive tribe, they pushed all before them causing a knock-on effect upon the various German tribes. The Vandals and Goths (until then occupying Poland and Silesia) were pushed west into the territory of the Saxons, Swabians and others. Many Saxons took sail for England while the Franks and Swabians crossed the Rhine into Roman Gaul. As the Huns continued west (under King Attila, they reached Gaul in AD451 although they soon disappeared from the scene after Attila's death), so the Vandals and Goths too were pushed into Roman-held lands in Austria, Switzerland and even Italy where the Goths sacked Rome in AD410. By then the Western Roman empire was under attack from all sides, eventually collapsing in AD476.

Western Europe was left with a patchwork of tribal nations, mostly descended from Germanic tribes. Not all Germans had participated in the migrations and those Saxons who had not crossed the North Sea to England became the dominant force in the lower Elbe basin. The Franks ended-up in France and under Charlemagne (ruled AD768–814) established the Carolingian empire which encompassed most of France, modern-day Germany and northern Italy. Charlemagne was crowned the first Holy Roman Emperor by Pope Leo III. After the death of his son, this empire was divided into three with the eastern Franks taking control of the land between the Rhine and Elbe. This area dubbed itself the 'Holy Roman Empire' (HRE), a strange title as it was a mixture of independent German states each with its own ruler who paid little more than lip service to the emperor. However, it was long-lasting and was still functioning eight centuries later, when Voltaire (1694–1778) called it 'neither Holy, nor Roman, nor an Empire'.

## Bohemia

Meanwhile, another set of migrations had started. The move west by Germanic tribes, the rapid departure of the Huns and the collapse of the Roman empire left large empty lands which attracted Slavic tribes to move west from Russia and Ukraine into Poland and Prussia. This occurred in three waves between AD550 and AD800. The Saxons in the Elbe valley prevented expansion west of the Elbe, so the Slavs turned south into the Czech and Slovak lands, Yugoslavia and Bulgaria.

A small Slavic tribe, the Přemyslids, settled in the Bohemian basin around what is now Prague. From the accession of Bořivoj I (AD867) they grew slowly more powerful. Their Bohemian empire reached its peak in the 14th century under Charles IV (1346–1378) who greatly expanded the country to include parts of Germany and Poland while founding Prague university and building Prague castle and St Vitus cathedral (Stage 6). Towards the end of the 15th century, marriage brought the Hungarian and Bohemian thrones together. When Louis II, King of Hungary and Bohemia, was killed fighting Ottoman Turkish invaders at the Battle of Mohacs (1526), there was no heir and the titles passed through his sister to her husband, the Habsburg Holy Roman Emperor, Ferdinand I. This was the end of independent Bohemia which was

*Charles bridge and Prague castle were built in the 14th century (Stage 6)*

absorbed into the Habsburg Austrian empire.

## The Habsburgs

Originally from Switzerland, the Habsburgs provided their first Holy Roman Emperor when Rudolf von Habsburg was elected in 1273 and moved his seat to Vienna. A series of dynastic marriages vastly expanded Habsburg influence and, from 1438 until Napoleon dissolved the HRE in 1805, they continuously occupied the imperial throne. After Bohemia's 1526 integration into the Habsburg Austrian empire, the country saw a gradual move away from religious tolerance towards a Catholic hegemony. Moreover, German influence grew as German migration was encouraged, so much so that by the 17th century Prague had a German-speaking majority.

## Saxony

After the dust had settled from the migrations, the Saxons were in control of the lands along the middle and lower Elbe. They were conquered by Charlemagne (AD804), eventually becoming part of East Francia and thus part of the HRE. Saxony was an important part of the empire and in 1356 it became an electorate, one of seven states ruled by an elector who between them chose the emperor. In 1485, a disputed succession led to partition into two states, Albertine Saxony ruled from Meissen by Duke Albert, and Ernestine Saxony ruled by Prince Ernst with its capital in Wittenberg. After moving their capital to Dresden, in 1547 the Albertines became the dominant branch. The heyday of Saxon Dresden was in the 18th century when the city was adorned with new palaces and cathedrals in Baroque and Rococo style, becoming known as the 'jewel box of Germany'. From 1756, when Saxony joined a coalition of Austria, France and Russia fighting Prussia and Britain in the Seven Years' War, the major adversary became their Prussian neighbours.

## Birth of Protestantism

Both Bohemia and Saxony experienced devastating civil wars between Protestants seeking to reform the established church and Catholics seeking to maintain the status quo. In Prague, a reformist preacher Jan Hus became rector of Charles university (1403) though he lost the king's support when he preached against the sale of indulgences, as the king took a percentage on all sales. Hus was summoned before the Catholic authorities at the Council of Constance where he was condemned as a heretic and burnt at the stake (1415). His death sparked civil war in Bohemia (1419–1434) between Protestant Hussites and Catholics. The war ended with a compromise promising freedom of religion. This held until 1620, when Catholic supremacy was reasserted after the Hussites were defeated at the Battle of White Mountain by

*Statue of Martin Luther in Wittenberg Marktplatz (Stage 15)*

combined forces of the HRE and Catholic League.

Just over 100 years after Hus's execution, Martin Luther, a Catholic monk and professor of theology at Wittenberg university in Saxony (Stage 15), published (1517) a letter of 95 theses attacking corrupt practices in the Catholic church, particularly the sale of indulgences. Luther was excommunicated by the Catholic authorities at the Diet of Worms (1521) and threatened with arrest and possible execution. However, he escaped and was given protection by Friedrich III, Elector of Saxony. He spent the rest of his life organising his Reformed church which quickly took hold in Saxony and was soon adopted by neighbouring German states. Despite defeat by the emperor's forces at the Battle of Mühlberg (1547), Protestantism was too deeply entrenched to be ended by force and in 1555 it gained equal status with Catholicism when rulers of German-speaking states were given the power to select one approved faith for their state.

### Thirty Years' War

This was the lull before the storm. When Catholic forces defeated Protestants in Bohemia (1620), rulers of north German Protestant states were outraged. War broke out, initially between Protestant and Catholic states within Germany but spread as neighbouring countries (including Spain, France, Netherlands, Denmark, Sweden and even Turkey) became involved. Relative to population size, the Thirty Years' War (1618–1648) was the most destructive in European history. Eight million people died, many of them civilians who died from starvation or disease caused by famine and pestilence. In some areas it was one hundred years before population regained pre-war levels. Many towns in the Elbe basin suffered during the war, particularly in Protestant Saxony where, for non-religious reasons, the Elector supported the Imperial (Catholic) forces rather than the Protestant league. When the Swedes entered the war on the Protestant side, they passed through Saxony destroying every town in sight. Although there

17

*Magdeburg town hall was rebuilt after destruction during the Thirty Years' War (Stage 18)*

were Catholic gains at first, by the time the war ended, the Protestants had the upper hand. The Peace of Westphalia (1648) made a few territorial changes, but more or less returned the states of the HRE to the same mixed religious status quo as pre-war.

## Napoleon and the Confederation of the Rhine

Germany remained a patchwork of states loosely attached to the HRE. Some were large, others very small, ruled by a collection of kings, princes, dukes, marquises, electors and even bishops. The catalyst for change came from outside. After disturbances caused by the French Revolution, Napoleon Bonaparte came to power in France (1799) and set off on a campaign to expand French power

in Europe. In 1805, victory over the Austrians and Russians at Austerlitz led to the dissolution of the HRE. This was followed in 1806 by victory over Prussia at the Battle of Jena. With most of Germany under French control, Napoleon swept away the old state boundaries and reorganised western Germany within a Confederation of the Rhine which eventually comprised 36 states including Saxony and Anhalt-Dessau in the Elbe basin. The Confederation was short-lived, and collapsed in 1813 after Napoleon was defeated at the Battle of Leipzig (much of the early campaigning took place in the area between Dresden and Leipzig covered by the route). However, it reshaped Germany, which was reborn after the war under two dominant states, Bavaria and Prussia. On the losing side, Saxon territory along the lower Elbe was annexed by Prussia, leaving Saxony much reduced in size.

## Prussia and the foundation of Germany

In 1594, the heir to the Hohenzollern Margraviate of Brandenburg married the daughter of the Duke of Prussia, paving the way for an eventual union of the states under Hohenzollern control. This happened in 1701 when Frederick III declared himself King of Prussia and moved the court from Königsberg to Berlin. Prussia established a standing army and small navy. Despite defeat by the French at Jena, the Prussians were strong enough to resist further French advances and maintain their independence. They played a major role in Napoleon's demise, first at Leipzig and then at Waterloo (1815), when allied British and Prussian armies ended his rule. The post-war congress of Vienna agreed a new structure for Germany. Many smaller states were amalgamated, becoming part of an enlarged Prussia, now a major European nation. In 1866, the Prussian-dominated North German Federation came into being and victory for Prussia in the Franco-Prussian War (1870–1871) brought Bavaria, Baden and Württemberg into a united Germany with the Prussian Hohenzollern ruler Wilhelm I as Kaiser (emperor).

## Growth of Czech nationalism

One of the effects of the French Revolution was to sow the seeds of

The national museum in Prague tells the story of the Czech National Revival movement (Stage 6)

nationalism throughout Europe. In Bohemia the Czech National Revival movement started campaigning for greater Bohemian autonomy and for Czech to replace German as the language of administration. In 1867, Hungary was given equal status within an Austro-Hungarian empire although an attempt to create the same rights for Bohemia in a tripartite monarchy was rebuffed. Nationalist support continued to grow, but it took the upheaval of a world war to bring independence to fruition.

## First World War and fall of the Habsburgs

The German and Austro-Hungarian empires fought together as the 'Central Powers' during the First World War (1914–1918). After defeat for this alliance, post-war treaties removed the Habsburgs from power and broke Austro-Hungary up into five new countries. One of these, intended as a homeland for Czech-speaking peoples, incorporated Bohemia with Moravia, Slovakia and Ruthenia into Czechoslovakia with Prague as its capital. Germany was stripped of its colonies and its borders were altered, though there was no effect on Saxony. The country was ordered to pay large reparations, which caused economic problems.

## Sudetenland and the Second World War

Economic and social turmoil in post-war Germany led to the growth of extremist political parties. The National Socialists (Nazis) led by Adolf Hitler exploited this unrest and came to power in 1933. Hitler objected to the terms of the post-war treaties and pursued a strategy of 'reuniting' German-speaking lands. He engineered a takeover of Austria (1936) and put pressure on Czechoslovakia over the rights of Sudeten Germans. This little-known group of people were ethnic Germans who had settled in the border regions of Bohemia (adjoining Saxony, Bavaria and Austria) while the country was part of, and integrated into, the Austrian empire. Though never before seen as a problem, the Nazis invaded Czechoslovakia (1938) to 'protect' their rights. Britain and France objected but did nothing after Hitler assured them that he had no further demands. When the Germans invaded Poland the following year, Britain and France declared war and the Second World War began. After German defeat in 1945, the Sudetens were expelled en masse from Czechoslovakia and went as refugees to Saxony (by then in East Germany) and Bavaria (West Germany). Over three million were expelled from towns including Vrchlabí (Stage 1) and Litoměřice (Stage 8).

The Nazis followed an extreme anti-Semitic doctrine aimed at eliminating Jewish people from Europe that resulted in the Holocaust. In Germany and occupied countries, including Czechoslovakia, Jews were first

*Nazi 'Work sets you free' slogan at Theresienstadt concentration camp (Stage 8)*

stripped of their rights, then confined in concentration camps including Theresienstadt (Stage 8). Some were used as slave labour in munitions and armaments factories while others were murdered; in total over six million were killed. These camps were also used to confine political prisoners and minority ethnic groups.

By 1944 the Allied powers (Britain, Russia and America) controlled the skies and mounted mass bombing raids using up to one thousand bombers against German industrial targets. The heaviest attacks in the Elbe basin were on Dresden (Stage 11) and Hamburg (Stage 26). During the final weeks of the war, American and British armies (from the west) and the Russian army (from the east) arrived simultaneously at the Elbe, where the first contact between eastern and western fronts occurred at Strehla (Stage 14) on 25 April 1945.

## Cold War divisions

Post-war Germany was divided into four sectors to be administered by the victorious Allied powers. The north, including Lower Saxony and Hamburg, was put first under British control then later united with the American and French sectors to become a free country in 1949. This flourished as the Bundes Republik Deutschland (BRD) and grew to become the most successful European economy.

The eastern sector was controlled by the Russians, who also kept control of Czechoslovakia. In both countries they set up Communist puppet states, that in East Germany being named the Deutsches Demokratische Republik (DDR). Private property was confiscated, state control was exercised over industrial companies, farms were collectivised and housing became state property. Investment was directed towards large state industrial projects and municipal housing often of poor-quality prefabricated high-rise apartment blocks. The 'Iron Curtain', a line of fences, barbed wire and minefields, was erected along the western border of both countries, allegedly to defend against western aggression but more accurately to prevent the population from leaving. An uprising against Communist control in Czechoslovakia (1968) was suppressed by the Russians. However, when poor economic performance led to renewed protests throughout eastern Europe (1989), the Russians did not intervene and the Communist system collapsed. East Germany was subsequently reunified with West Germany (1990), while Czechoslovakia became an independent nation. In 1993, a peaceful split between the Czech and Slovak parts of the country saw two new countries created, the Czech Republic (now Czechia) and Slovakia.

## European Union

West Germany, which signed the treaty of Rome (1957) was a founder member of the EU. East Germany automatically joined the EU after reunification (1990) while Czechia joined in 2004. Both countries have signed the Schengen agreement providing open borders between them and their neighbours.

## NATURAL ENVIRONMENT

### Physical geography

The Elbe rises in the thickly forested Krkonoše mountains. Formed of granite, the range is the highest part of Czechia and part of the Sudeten highlands that lie along the country's

*Preserved section of Iron Curtain fencing at Dömitz (Stage 23)*

*The Elbe rises in Czechia's Krkonoše mountains (Stage 1)*

northern border with Poland. South of the mountains, the river flows through the fertile central Bohemian basin (Stages 3–8) before turning north again following a deep gorge (Stages 9–11) through another part of the Sudeten highlands, the basalt České Středohoří. This was formed about five million years ago when a chain of volcanoes broke through the underlying sandstone of the basin. This gorge continues through the Elbesandsteingebirge (known as Saxon Switzerland), the most geologically scenic part of the Elbe valley, where the sandstone has been raised up then eroded by wind and water into fantastic rock formations of pinnacles and bridges.

Emerging from the mountains, the Elbe reaches the North German plain (Stages 12–25), a vast flat region formed by the advance and retreat of the Scandinavian ice-sheet during the Pleistocene period (2,500,000BC–12,000BC), which is composed mainly of loess (wind-blown soil) and river-borne sediment. The river winds its way sedately across this plain, descending only 100m in 600km. As a result it has been prone to regular flooding, a trait which mankind has attempted to control by straightening the course and building dykes and flood barriers. Originally covered by beech forest, this area has been cleared during ten thousand years of human habitation to become fertile farmland for both arable and pastoral products. A few low hills, mostly the remnants of former moraines, dot the plain. These often form the base for a

*Sheep are used as natural lawnmowers to keep the grass short on flood dykes (Stage 23)*

town rising slightly above the riverside flood meadows.

The final 150km before reaching the North Sea (Stages 26–29) is an area originally formed of salt-marsh and swamp, much of it close to or below sea level. This has been reclaimed since the 12th century, with sluice gates and pumping stations keeping the sea out, and it now forms some of Germany's most fertile farmland producing fruit, vegetables and dairy products.

## Wildlife

Several small mammals and reptiles (including rabbits, hares, squirrels and snakes) may be encountered scuttling across the track, and deer can be seen in forests and fields. In most of Germany, Eurasian beaver were hunted to extinction during the 19th century, although a small population survived on the Elbe. Conservation measures to prevent hunting and preserve habitat have resulted in over 6000 specimens on the Elbe today, together with many that have been trans-located to reintroduce beavers to other parts of the country.

The most unusual animal you might see is the *waschbär* (American raccoon). In 1945 about two dozen animals escaped from a fur farm in Brandenburg and became feral. Their natural habitat is forested wetland and they spread along the Spree and Havel rivers to reach the Elbe. Rapid population growth since 2000 has resulted in over 250,000 animals in the Spree, Havel and Elbe systems. The raccoon is now classed as an undesirable species and free hunting is allowed with 50,000 being caught annually. Although they are nocturnal, raccoons are sometimes seen during the day between Havelberg and Wittenberge (Stage 22).

Another conservation success is the white stork. These large birds nest in trees or on man-made platforms and hunt frogs, toads and rodents in riverside meadows. Decline during the first half of the 20th century, mostly due to changes in land use and hydrological engineering, was less pronounced in eastern Germany than in the west, and the Elbe basin is home to 25 per cent of Germany's 4000 breeding pairs. Numbers are

*Storks' nest on St Laurentii church in Frohse (Stage 18)*

stable and the bird is no longer regarded as a threatened species.

Although not wild animals, large flocks of sheep are used as natural lawnmowers to keep the grass short on flood dykes. They are kept in designated areas by electric fences which are moved every few days along the dyke.

## THE ROUTE

From the source of the Elbe at Pramen Labe high in the Krkonoše mountains (part of the Sudetenland), the Elbe cycleway (Labská Stezka in Czech, Elberadweg in German) runs 1227km to Cuxhaven, a port on the German North Sea coast. The river flows initially south, first descending 900m steeply through small ski resorts and wooded forests to Vrchlabí (Stage 1), then gently down through the foothills to Hostinné and Jaroměř (Stage 2) and almost level through Hradec Králové to the navigable head of the river at Pardubice (Stage 3). Here the river turns west through central Bohemia where the cycle route (Stages 4–5) passes through agricultural countryside with many small villages. Stages 6–7 provide an opportunity to leave the Elbe for a brief visit to the great Bohemian city of Prague, while Stage 7A allows purists to follow the river, by-passing the city's delights by following the river through the central Bohemian plain.

After Prague, the river makes its last major change in direction and

*The route follows the river Vltava north from Prague (Stage 7)*

now flows north west all the way to the North Sea. Stages 8–11 take the route through another part of the Sudetenland mountain chain, this time following a deep and attractive gorge past towering sandstone spires and heavily forested slopes known in Czechia as the 'Porta Bohemica' and in Germany as 'Saxon Switzerland'. There are a series of riverside towns, some are Bohemian jewels like Litoměřice and Děčín, while others are industrial centres like Ústí nad Labem. In Stage 10 the route leaves Czechia and enters Germany, leaving the mountains behind to reach Dresden, the historic capital of Saxony (Stage 11).

Continuing north west through former East Germany, the almost relentlessly flat route (Stages 12–15)

follows the river through agricultural countryside and a series of small/medium-sized towns like Meissen, Riesa and Torgau to reach Wittenberg-Lutherstadt in Saxony Anhalt. Here the river makes a long loop to the west to avoid the Hoher Fläming hills, passing Dessau to reach the industrial city of Magdeburg (Stages 16–18).

Continuing north (Stages 19–21), still in Saxony Anhalt, the Elbe passes Tangermünde to reach Havelberg on an island in the river Havel surrounded by low-lying water meadows where the Havel joins the Elbe. The route now runs north west mostly along flood dykes, first passing Wittenberge and Dömitz (Stages 22–23) beside the former line of the Iron Curtain (a couple of watchtowers are all that remain), then crossing the river into Lower Saxony, previously part of West Germany. A series of attractive towns are passed (Hitzacker, Bleckede and Lauenburg) (Stages 24–25) before reaching tidal water at Geesthacht. The Vierlande, a drained former marshland now used to grow vegetables for the Hamburg market, is crossed following the route of an old railway (Stage 26) before the river is closely followed through Hamburg, Germany's second largest city.

The final stretch (Stages 27–29) crosses more former marshland of the Altes Land, now Germany's largest fruit-growing area, to reach the attractive fishing port town of Stade. It then continues across the Kehdingen salt marshes alongside the Elbe estuary to Cuxhaven, a major fishing port and resort town by the river mouth.

## PREPARATION

### When to go

The route is best followed between May and October when there are longer days with warmer weather and no chance of snow. Most ferries have shorter working periods in the winter and some do not run at all. The Medvědin chairlift (prologue) only carries cycles in summer.

### How long will it take?

The route has been broken into 29 stages averaging 42km/stage. A fit cyclist, riding 82km/day (51 miles) should be able to complete the route in 15 days, while a faster cyclist averaging 95km/day (60 miles) could do it in 13 days. A more leisurely pace of 65km/day (40 miles) should

*Havelberg sits on an island in the river Havel (Stage 21)*

accomplish the ride in 19 days. Some possible schedules appear at the front of this guide, but as there are many places to stay it is easy to tailor daily distances to your own requirements.

## What kind of cycle is suitable?

Most of the route is on surfaced roads or cycle tracks although there are sections of gravel track and some unsurfaced stretches. The most suitable cycles are hybrids, tourers or trail bikes. Road bikes would struggle with some of the surfaces and mountain bikes are unnecessary as gradients and going are very gentle. Front suspension is beneficial as it absorbs much of the vibration. Straight handlebars, with bar-ends enabling you to vary your position regularly, are recommended. Make sure your cycle is serviced and lubricated before you start, particularly the brakes, gears and chain.

As important as the cycle, is your choice of tyres. You need a good quality touring tyre with a deeper tread and a slightly wider profile than you would use for everyday cycling. Knobbly mountain bike tyres are not suitable. To reduce the chance of punctures, choose tyres with puncture resistant armouring, such as a Kevlar™ band.

## GETTING THERE AND BACK

### Getting to the start

It is possible to reach Vrchlabí, the nearest station to the Elbe spring, in a day from the UK by air, but not by train. As a result, most people choose

*The riverside cycle track near Týnec nad Labem is unsurfaced (Stage 4)*

to fly with their cycles to Prague rather than spending two days on trains.

Eight different airlines operate direct flights between various UK airports and Prague. Airlines have different requirements regarding how cycles are presented and some, but not all, make a charge which you should pay when booking as it is usually greater at the airport. All require tyres partially deflated, handlebars turned and pedals removed (loosen pedals beforehand to make them easier to remove at the airport). Most will accept your cycle in a transparent polythene bike bag, though some insist on the use of a cardboard bike box. Cycling UK (formerly the Cyclists' Touring Club, CTC) have designed a polythene bike bag which can be obtained from Wiggle, www.wiggle. co.uk. Cardboard bike boxes can be obtained from most cycle shops, often for free. However, you do have the problem of getting your box to the airport. If flying through Heathrow, Gatwick or Luton, airport branches of Excess Baggage Company, www. excess-baggage.com, sell bike boxes for £35. At Gatwick, the main warehouse of Evans Cycles, www. evanscycles.com, which always has bike boxes, is near the airport only 10 minutes' ride from the South Terminal building.

If you fly into Prague you will need to reach Prague Hlavní station in order to catch a train to Vrchlabí. It is 16km from airport to station, mostly on or beside busy highways.

However, Prague airport express buses (Route AE), which run directly from the airport to Hlavní, are one of only two bus services in Prague which carry cycles. If your bike is boxed for air transportation carriage is free, otherwise you pay a single fare for the bike. So, if you arrive with your bike packed, it is best to take it on by bus to Hlavní before unpacking it.

From Praha Hlavní, inter-city trains which carry cycles run two-hourly through Chlumec nad Cidlinou, from where a local stopping train will take you to Kunčice nad Labem. Finally, it is a short journey by branch line train to Vrchlabí. Journey time from Prague Hlavní is approximately 3 hours. Booking at www. cd.cz. Czech country stations mostly have very low (or no!) platforms and you will find it easier to lift your bike on and off the train if you remove your panniers. Travel websites like seat61. com and trainline.eu are also useful when planning travel.

### Intermediate access

There are international airports at Prague (Stage 6) and Hamburg (Stage 25) with direct flights from various UK cities. There are no direct flights from the UK to Dresden (Stage 11) but it can be reached using connecting flights. Berlin (Brandenburg) is approximately 90km from Wittenberg (Stage 15) .

In Czechia, the river is closely followed by railway lines and there are frequent stations near the route.

Loading cycles on Czech trains can sometimes be a challenge (Stage 1)

In Germany the situation is different. Although most stage-end towns have a station, this is usually on a line crossing the river or at the end of a branch line. Apart from the first stage from Bad Schandau to Dresden (Stage 11) there are no railways that follow the river and as a result very few of the smaller towns and villages on the cycleway have stations.

Apart from high-speed ICE trains in Germany and some long-distance inter-city trains in Czechia, almost all trains in both countries have bicycle spaces. In Czechia, passenger fares are extremely low, although a flat fare of 30Kč (Czech koruna) is applied to bicycle transportation. This provides 150km of travel, beyond which bicycles are charged a fee based upon distance travelled. In both countries a cycle day ticket is needed to use local and regional trains. Cycle space on long-distance trains needs to be reserved.

**Getting home**

If you wish to fly home at the end of your ride, the nearest international airport is Hamburg. To reach Hamburg airport from Cuxhaven, RE5 regional express trains operate hourly between Cuxhaven and Hamburg Hbf, from where frequent S1 S-Bahn trains, destination Hamburg Flughafen, serve the airport. A cycle day ticket (€3.50) is needed for the RE train. Cycles are carried free on the S-Bahn, but not during weekday peak hours (0600–0900 and 1600–1800). These restrictions do not apply during Hamburg summer holidays, from late June to early August.

If you are returning to the UK by train, London can be reached in a long day from Cuxhaven. The journey needs careful planning as neither German ICE high-speed trains nor Thalys trains that operate between Germany and Belgium carry cycles. An early morning departure from Cuxhaven to either Hamburg Harburg or Bremen via Bremerhaven will connect with an inter-city train to Köln. From here a regional train will take you to Aachen, then a local train makes the short 15-minute hop over the Belgian border to Welkenraedt. An hourly Belgian inter-city train will take you to Brussels from where two-hourly Eurostar services connect with London. Total journey time is approximately 12 hours.

Booking for German trains can be made through www.bahn.com, where advance booking often gives a very good price for a through ticket from Cuxhaven to Aachen, including a cycle reservation. When using www.bahn.com, click 'further options' and then 'carriage of bicycle' to see only trains with cycle space. SNCB Belgian tickets can be booked at www.belgiantrain.be. A €5 single-journey cycle ticket is required for the train from Welkenraedt to Brussels.

Eurostar tickets can be booked up to six months in advance at www.eurostar.com, A separate reservation needs to be obtained for your cycle which cannot be done online and must be made by phone (0344 822 5822) or by email to EuroDespatch@

eurostar.com. There are six cycle spaces on every train, two for fully assembled bikes and four for disassembled bikes packed in a special fibreglass case provided by Eurostar. Prices vary from £30–£55 depending on how far ahead you book. and whether the bike is fully assembled or disassembled. Bikes need to be delivered to 'Bagages' at Brussels Midi station (just off main concourse beside passageway to Platform 6) one hour before train departure time (90 minutes for a disassembled bike as you will need time to pack it; Eurostar will provide the tools). On arrival at London St Pancras, cycles can be collected from EuroDespatch at the back of the station beside the coach drop-off area.

## NAVIGATION

### Waymarking
The route is well waymarked throughout. In Czechia Stages 1–5, 7A and 8–10 follow Czech National Cycle Route 2, while Stages 6–7 via Prague follow national routes 17 and 7 plus Prague regional routes A26 and A2. In Germany the route is waymarked as Elberadweg which usually coincides with German National Cycle Route D10.

### Maps
It is possible to cycle the route using only the maps in this book. If you want more detailed mapping, Public

Press (www.publicpress.de) publish a series of three laminated strip maps at a scale of 1:50,000 covering the route through Germany: Bad Schandau–Dessau (ISBN 978-3-89920-448-3), Dessau–Wittenberge (978-3-89920-242-7) and Wittenberge–Cuxhaven (9783899202748).

An interactive online map can be found on the official Elberadweg website (www.elbe-cycle-route.com) while www.openstreetmap.org has a cycle-map option which shows the route in relation to its surroundings and facilities.

### GPX tracks

GPX tracks for the routes in this guidebook are available to download free at www.cicerone.co.uk/1055/GPX. If you have not bought the book through the Cicerone website, or have bought the book without opening an account, please register your purchase in your Cicerone library to access GPX and update information.

A GPS device is an excellent aid to navigation, but you should also carry a map and compass and know how to use them. GPX files are provided in good faith, but in view of the profusion of formats and devices, neither the author nor the publisher accepts responsibility for their use. We provide files in a single standard GPX format that works on most devices and systems, but you may need to convert files to your preferred format using a GPX converter such as gpsvisualizer.com or one of the many other apps and online converters available.

### Guidebooks

The combined tourist development bodies of Bohemia and the four German *länder* along the Elberadweg have produced an official handbook. This free publication, which is updated annually, has 100 pages listing cycle-friendly accommodation, refreshment opportunities and cycle shops, with rudimentary maps. The guide is published in German, Czech or Dutch but an English translation of the key elements (but not the listings) is available. It can be ordered online (www.elbe-cycle-route.com) or can be picked up at tourist offices en route.

## ACCOMMODATION

On most stages there is a wide variety of places to overnight, ranging from campsites through youth hostels, bed and breakfasts, guest houses and local inns to five-star hotels. Tourist information offices can provide lists of local accommodation in all categories. Booking ahead is seldom necessary, except in high season (July

**Waymarking (opposite: clockwise from top):** *Czech cyclists' fingerpost; Czech national cycle route waymark; German fingerpost; a local signpost in Steckby (Stage 17); German Elberadweg and D10 waymark*

*Czech 'Cyclists welcome' sign*

*German 'Bed+Bike' sign*

and August) but it is advisable to start looking for accommodation soon after 1600. Cycle-friendly establishments within 2.5km of the route that meet six criteria (single-night accommodation, secure cycle storage, drying facilities, cycle repair equipment, breakfast provided and packed lunch available) are allowed to display an *Elberadweg radfreundliche unterkunft* (cycle-friendly accommodation) sign or a Czech 'Cyclists welcome' sign and are listed in the official handbook. The stage descriptions identify places known to have accommodation, but the list is not exhaustive.

**Hotels and guest houses**
Hotels and inns usually offer a full meal service, guest houses do sometimes. B&Bs, which in Germany can be recognised by a sign *zimmer frei* (rooms available), generally offer only breakfast. Tourist information offices will normally telephone for you and make local reservations. If you use a search engine, booking.com has a wide range of accommodation in Germany and Czechia. In Czechia, prices for all kinds of accommodation are lower than in the UK, while in Germany prices are similar to the UK.

Bett+Bike (www.bettundbike.de) is a German scheme run by ADFC (German national cycling club), which has registered over 5000 establishments providing cycle-friendly accommodation. It includes a wide variety of properties, from major hotels to local B&Bs, listed by state in an annually updated guidebook. Participating establishments display a Bett+Bike sign.

**Youth hostels**
There are 23 official youth hostels, some in historic buildings, on or near the route (5 Czech, 18 German), though as some cities have more than

*Strehla youth hostel is in an old windmill (Stage 14)*

one, there are 17 towns/cities with hostels. They are reasonably well spread but there are none in the first six stages until Prague and none on Stages 19–24 between Magdeburg and Hitzacker. All hostels are listed in Appendix C. Czech hostels are open to all-comers with a 10 per cent discount for members of an association affiliated to Hostelling International (YHA in England/Wales, SYHA in Scotland). To use a German hostel you need to be an HI affiliated association member, though if you are not you will be able to purchase a guest card. Visitors over 27 must pay a €3 surcharge. Rooms vary from single-sex dormitories to family rooms of two to six beds. Most continental European hostels do not have self-catering facilities but provide good-value hot meals. Hostels get very busy, particularly during school holidays, and booking is advised through www.hihostels.com.

## Camping

There are many official campsites along the route and locations are shown in the route descriptions. Campsites are generally well equipped and maintained. In some you can hire a cabin, a popular way of holidaying during the Communist period. Wild camping is illegal in Czechia and most German states.

## FOOD AND DRINK

### Where to eat

There are many places where cyclists can eat and drink, varying from snack bars, hotdog stands and local inns

35

to Michelin-starred restaurants. The route is dotted with small restaurants/cafés/bars that provide lunchtime sustenance for cyclists, usually with a row of cycle racks outside. Locations of many places to eat are listed in stage descriptions, but these are not exhaustive. Days and times of opening vary. When planning your day, try to be flexible as a many inns and small restaurants do not open at lunchtime and usually have one day a week (*ruhetag*) when they remain closed. A local inn offering food and drink is typically known as a *hospoda* (Czech) or *gaststätte* (German), while a wine bar is a *vinárny* (Czech) or *weinstube* (German). English-language menus are often available in big cities and tourist areas, but are less common elsewhere.

If you prefer a picnic lunch, all towns and many villages have both a bakery and a grocery. There are frequent cyclist rest areas, usually a roofed shelter with cycle parking facilities, where you can consume your picnic. Some even have a free pump for your tyres!

### When to eat
Breakfast (German *frühstück*, Czech *snídaně*) is usually continental; it normally consists of breads, jam and a hot drink with the optional addition of cold meats, cheese and a boiled egg. Traditionally lunch (German *mittagessen*, Czech *oběd*) was the main meal of the day, but this is slowly changing, and is likely to prove unsuitable

if you plan an afternoon in the saddle. The most common lunchtime snacks everywhere are soups and salads. For dinner (German *abendessen*, Czech *večeře*) a wide variety of cuisine is available. Portions tend to be large, particularly in Germany. Much of what is available is pan-European and will be easily recognisable. There are, however, national and regional dishes you may wish to try.

### What to eat
Most Czech meals start with *polévka* (soup), either a bouillon or a hearty

**Top:** Svíčková *(beef sirloin served with sour cream, cranberries and dumplings) is popular in Czechia;* **Bottom:** Soljanka *is a hearty meat and vegetable soup, popular in eastern Germany since Soviet times*

mix made from potatoes, vegetables and some meat. Popular main courses include *pečené vepřové* (roast pork), *svíčková* (marinated beef sirloin) and *guláš* (spicy meat stew). Roast meat is often served with a thick cream-based sauce, *knedliky* (dumplings) and *zelim* (cabbage). *Kuře* (chicken), often served in paprika sauce (*kuře na paprice*), and *kachna* (duck) are widely available. *Pstruh* (trout) is the most popular fish; most other types of fish are imported. *Palačinky* (pancakes) and *buchtičky* (sweet dumplings) are frequently served desserts.

Germany is the land of the *schwein* (pig) with pork, gammon, bacon and ham dishes dominating menus. Pork specialities in eastern Germany include *Königsbergerklopse* (pork meatballs in a creamy sauce with capers and lemon, usually served with boiled potatoes), *eisbein* (roasted pork knuckle served with sauerkraut and dumplings, known in western Germany as *schweinhaxe*) and *sülze* (jellied pressed pork served with pickles and raw onion). Schnitzels are thin escalopes, usually pork but can be veal, that are breadcrumbed and fried. *Soljanka* is a hearty meat and vegetable soup usually filling enough to provide a light lunch. It originated in Ukraine and was introduced into East Germany during the Communist era. Unlike most things Soviet, it became popular and has survived the fall of Communism.

There are many types of German *wurst* (sausage), the most common

being *bratwurst* (made from minced pork and served grilled or fried), *wienerwurst* (smoked sausages served boiled, known as frankfurters in English) and *blutwurst* (black pudding). *Currywurst* are sausages smothered with a mild curry sauce and usually served with chips. *Sauerbraten* is marinated roast beef, while *fleischkäse* and *leberkäse* are kinds of meat loaf. *Forelle* (trout), *lachs* (salmon) and *zander* (pike-perch) are the most popular fish. In Cuxhaven (Stage 29), which is one of Europe's largest fishing ports, there is a whole street of restaurants serving every imaginable type of freshly caught fish.

The most common vegetable accompaniments are sauerkraut and boiled potatoes. *Reibekuchen* are potato pancakes, sometimes served with apple sauce. *Spargel* (white asparagus) is consumed in huge quantities during *spargelzeit* (asparagus season), between mid April and 24 June.

Germans tend to consume cakes (*kuchen*) and sweet products with coffee mid morning or late afternoon and not as part of a main meal. As a result, desserts are rather limited, often just apple strudel or ice cream.

### What to drink
Czechia and Germany are traditionally beer- (Czech *pivo*, German *bier*) drinking nations, indeed they are the first and fourth largest countries in the world ranked by consumption per head. Bohemia was the

origin of pilsener-style beer which gets its name from the town of Plzeň in western Bohemia. Budweiser Budvar was first brewed in 1265 in České Budějovice, while Budweiser beer in America (first brewed 1876) is a copy of the original. Budweiser Budvar, Urquell (from Plzeň) and Staropramen (Prague) are the three largest breweries in Czechia, though in recent years there has been a growth in the number of micro-breweries and brew-pubs producing craft beers in *svělte* (pale) or *tmave* (dark) varieties. Strength is measured in degrees rather than by per cent ABV (alcohol by volume), with 10° being equivalent to 4%ABV and 12° equivalent to 5%ABV.

In Germany, purity laws controlling the production and content of beer have limited the mass consolidation of brewing compared to other European countries, beer being brewed in a large number of local breweries. Pilsener is the most widely drunk form, although other styles are growing in popularity. These include *weizenbier* (wheat beer), found in both *helles* (pale) and *dunkles* (dark) varieties, and *kellerbier*, an unpasteurised naturally cloudy beer with a similar taste to English bitter ale. Glass sizes vary, but common sizes are *kleines* (small, 300ml) and *grosses* (large, half litre). *Radler* (shandy) is a 50/50 mix of beer and carbonated lemonade while *diesel* is 50/50 beer and cola.

Although there are a few small vineyards in the Czech Elbe valley around Mělník (Stage 7), 90 per cent of Czech wine is produced in Moravia in the south of the country. Likewise, while there are vineyards around Dresden almost all German wine comes from the Rhine, Moselle and Main valleys in western Germany. Most wine in both countries is white from müller-thurgau, grüner veltliner

*Riverside restaurants abound, like this one near Kolín (Stage 5)*

or riesling grapes, with a small volume of soft reds produced from *blauburgunder* (German for pinot noir) grapes.

In Czechia, Becherovka, Fernet Stock (herbal infusions usually consumed as an aperitif) and *slivovice* (plum brandy) are the most popular local spirits. In Germany schnapps fruit brandies made with apples, pears, cherries, apricots or plums are the major spirits.

All the usual soft drinks (colas, lemonade, fruit juices, mineral waters) are available. Kofola (Czechia) and Vita Cola (former East Germany) are cola-style drinks introduced during Communist times to replace Coca-Cola, which have remained popular. Raspberry-flavoured lemonade, often served on draught, is the most common soft drink in Czechia. In Germany, *saftschorle* is fruit juice mixed 50/50 with carbonated water; *apfelschorle* (apple) and *rhabarberschorle* (rhubarb) are the most popular. Tap water is safe to drink throughout the route.

## AMENITIES AND SERVICES

### Grocery shops
All cities, towns and larger villages passed through have grocery stores, often supermarkets, and most have pharmacies. Opening hours vary, but grocers in Germany close at 1300 on Saturdays and stay closed all day Sunday.

### Cycle shops
Most towns have cycle shops with repair facilities equipped to repair and service all types of bike. Many will adjust brakes and gears, lubricate your chain or make minor repairs while you wait. Cycle shop locations are shown in stage descriptions, though this list is not exhaustive.

### Currency and banks
Germany switched from Deutsche marks to euros (€) in 2002. Czechia uses koruna (crowns), though a change to euros, originally planned for 2010, has been postponed indefinitely. The exchange rate is approximately 25 koruna to €1.

Almost every town has a bank and most have ATM machines which enable you to make transactions in English. However, very few offer over-the-counter currency exchange and the only way to obtain currency is to use ATM machines to withdraw cash from your personal account or from a prepaid travel card. Contact your bank to activate your bank card for use in Europe or put cash on a travel card. Credit or debit cards can be used for most purchases. Travellers' cheques are rarely used.

### Telephone and internet
The whole route has mobile phone (*handy* in German) coverage. Contact your network provider to ensure your phone is enabled for foreign use with the optimum price package. International dialling codes are

*Cycling past a cyclist mural at Büttnershof (Stage 21)*

+44 for UK, +420 for Czechia and +49 for Germany.

Almost all hotels, guest houses, hostels and many restaurants make internet access available to guests, usually free.

### Electricity

Czechia and Germany both use standard European two-pin round plugs. Voltage is 220v, 50HzAC.

## WHAT TO TAKE

### Clothing and personal items

Although the route is generally flat, weight should be kept to a minimum. You will need clothes for cycling (shoes, socks, shorts/trousers, shirt, fleece, waterproofs) and clothes for evenings and days off. The best maxim is two of each, 'one to wear, one to wash'. Time of year makes a difference as you need more and warmer clothing in April/May and September/October, when gloves and a woolly hat are advisable for cold morning starts. A sun-hat and sun glasses are essential. All of this clothing should be capable of washing en route, and a small tube or bottle of travel wash is useful.

In addition to your usual toiletries you will need sun cream and lip salve. You should take a simple first-aid kit. If staying in youth hostels, you will need a towel and torch (your cycle light should suffice).

### Cycle equipment

Everything you take needs to be carried on your cycle. If overnighting in accommodation, a pair of rear panniers should be sufficient to carry all your clothing and equipment, though if camping, you may also need front panniers. Panniers should be 100 per cent watertight. If in doubt, pack everything inside a strong polythene lining bag. Rubble bags, obtainable from builders' merchants are ideal for this purpose. A bar-bag is a useful way of carrying items you need to access quickly such as maps, sunglasses, camera, spare tubes, puncture kit and tools. A transparent map case attached to the top of your bar-bag is an ideal way of displaying maps and guidebook.

Your cycle should be fitted with mudguards and bell. It should be capable of carrying water bottles and pump. Lights are required if cycling at night. Many cyclists fit an odometer to measure distances. A basic tool kit should consist of puncture repair kit, spanners, Allen keys, adjustable spanner, screwdriver, spoke key and chain repair tool. The only essential spares are two spare tubes. On a long cycle ride your chain will need regular lubrication and you should either carry a can of spray-lube or make regular visits to cycle shops. A strong lock is advisable. Helmets are recommended but are not legally required for adults in Germany or Czechia.

## SAFETY AND EMERGENCIES

### Weather

The first part of the route as far as Magdeburg (Stage 18) is in the continental climate zone with warm summers, cold winters and moderate precipitation of rain in summer and snow in winter, though weather at the beginning of the first stage is affected by the mountains where snow can lie until mid May. After Magdeburg, the climate becomes progressively more oceanic, influenced by proximity to the North Sea. Temperatures are less extreme with slightly cooler summers and slightly warmer winters with year-round moderate rain. Prevailing westerly winds can produce annoyingly strong headwinds on the stages after Hamburg (Stages 27–29).

| Average temperatures (max/min degrees °C) | | | | | | | |
|---|---|---|---|---|---|---|---|
| | Apr | May | June | July | Aug | Sep | Oct |
| Prague | 15/3 | 20/9 | 22/11 | 25/13 | 24/13 | 19/9 | 13/5 |
| Dresden | 14/4 | 19/9 | 22/12 | 24/14 | 24/14 | 19/10 | 14/7 |
| Hamburg | 12/3 | 18/7 | 20/11 | 22/13 | 22/13 | 18/10 | 13/6 |

| Average rainfall (mm/rainy days) | | | | | | | |
|---|---|---|---|---|---|---|---|
| | Apr | May | June | July | Aug | Sep | Oct |
| Prague | 38/7 | 77/10 | 73/10 | 66/9 | 70/9 | 40/7 | 31/6 |
| Dresden | 41/9 | 65/9 | 65/11 | 87/10 | 83/9 | 50/8 | 43/6 |
| Hamburg | 43/9 | 57/10 | 79/11 | 77/11 | 79/10 | 67/11 | 67/11 |

Preserved windmill at Gohlis (Stage 12)

### Road safety

In Czechia and Germany cycling is on the right side of the road. If you have never cycled before on the right you will quickly adapt, but roundabouts may prove challenging. You are most prone to mistakes when setting off each morning. Both countries are very cycle-friendly. Drivers will normally give you space when overtaking and often wait behind patiently until room to pass is available.

Many city and town centres have pedestrian-only zones. These restrictions are often loosely enforced and you may find locals cycling within them, indeed many zones have signs allowing cycling. One-way streets often have signs permitting contra-flow cycling although in some cases you will need to dismount and walk your cycle.

### Health

No special injections or health precautions are needed, though it is advisable to make sure basic inoculations for tetanus, diphtheria and hepatitis are up to date. The greatest health risk comes from sunshine and heat. Sun hat, sunscreen, and lip salve are recommended.

### Emergencies

In the unlikely event of an accident, the standardised EU emergency phone number is 112. The entire route has mobile phone coverage. Provided you have an EHIC card issued by an EU or EFTA country, or a UK GHIC card, medical costs are covered under reciprocal health insurance agreements, although you may have to pay for an ambulance and claim the cost back through insurance.

### Theft

In general, the route is safe and the risk of theft low. However, you should always lock your cycle and watch your belongings, especially in cities.

### Insurance

Travel insurance policies usually cover you when cycle touring but they do not normally cover damage to, or theft of, your bicycle. If you have a household contents policy, this may cover cycle theft, but limits may be less than the actual cost of your cycle. Cycling UK, formerly known as the Cyclists' Touring Club (CTC) offer a policy tailored to the needs of cycle tourists www.cyclinguk.org.

## USING THIS GUIDE

### Text and maps

There are 29 main stages and one alternative, each covered by separate maps drawn to a scale of 1:150,000.

All places names shown in bold in the text appear on the maps. Distances shown are cumulative kilometres within each stage. For each city/town/village passed an indication is given of facilities available (accommodation, refreshments, youth hostel, camping, tourist office, cycle shop, station) when the guide was written. This indication is neither exhaustive nor does it guarantee that establishments are still in business. Tourist information offices (Appendix B) and youth hostels (Appendix C) are listed in full though no attempt has been made to list other facilities as this would require another book the same size as this one. For a full listing of accommodation, contact local tourist offices. Such listings are usually available online.

Gradient profiles are provided for Stages 1, 2, 6 and 7 which have significant ascents or descents. Ascents and descents on other stages are minimal.

Whilst route descriptions were accurate at the time of writing, things do change. Temporary diversions may be necessary to circumnavigate improvement works and permanent diversions to incorporate new sections of track. Where construction is in progress you may find signs showing recommended diversions, though these are likely to be in local languages.

Abbreviations used in the route description are L (left), R (right) and sp (signposted).

### Language

Czech is spoken in Czechia and German in Germany. Since the ethno-linguistic expulsions in 1945 there is no overlap of day-to-day languages though German is generally understood in Czech tourist locations.

This guide is written for an English-speaking readership. Along the route, most people working in the tourist industry speak at least a few words of English, but it is not widely used in rural areas and smaller towns. Any attempt to speak Czech or German is usually warmly appreciated.

In the text, Czech names are used in Czechia and German ones in Germany. The Elbe is described as the Labe in Czechia and becomes the Elbe when it reaches Germany in Stage 10. There are a few exceptions where English names are used for Prague (Praha), and the *länder* (German regions) of Saxony (Sachsen), Saxony-Anhalt (Sachsen-Anhalt) and Lower Saxony (Niedersachsen). The German 'ß' (known as an *eszett*), is shown as 'ss'. When this is followed by a word starting with 's', it can lead to a triple 'sss' appearing as in Schlossstrasse (Castle Street). In German, descriptive adjectives preceding a noun are usually closed up to form a compound word. A basic language glossary (English/Czech/German) can be found in Appendix F.

# THE ROUTE

_The Elbe cycle route begins by crossing open moorland in the Krkonoše mountains (Stage 1)_

# PROLOGUE
## Vrchlabí to Elbe spring

| | |
|---|---|
| **Start** | Vrchlabí station (467m) |
| **Finish** | Labská bouda (1340m) (1km walk to Elbe spring) |
| **Distance** | 24.5km (plus 2km by chairlift) |
| **Ascent** | 588m (plus 490m by chairlift) |
| **Descent** | 205m |
| **Waymarking** | Czech National Cycle Route 2 to Špindlerův Mlýn, then none |

From Vrchlabí there are two routes to reach the source of the Elbe at Pramen Labe (Elbe spring) in the Krkonoše (Giant) mountains. One climbs steeply on quiet mountain roads and forest tracks ascending over 1000m, the other follows a main road gently ascending the Labe valley then uses a chairlift to climb nearly 500m into the mountains. This prologue uses the main road/chairlift route to reach the source while the next stage (Stage 1) descends following the alternative road/forest track route back through Vrchlabí. You can leave your panniers in Vrchlabí and cycle up to the source unencumbered, collecting them on the way back.

For route map see Stage 1.

The Labe is the Czech name for the Elbe and this is your first sight of the river.

◄ From front of **Vrchlabí** station (467m) cycle ahead away from station on Kpt Otakara Jaroše. Turn R at crossroads (Dělnická) then L at roundabout (third exit, Tyršova, sp Praha). Cross river Labe and turn R (Českých bratří). ◄ Keep R at fork, then bear L (Nádražní) following one-way system. Turn R at crossroads (Krkonošská) and cycle through town centre. Pass Sv Vavřinec church R and turn immediately R (Ulice 5, Května) then turn second L (Ulice J K Tyla). Dog-leg L and R across main road past small factory R and at end turn R on narrow gravel track behind factory. Continue beside Labe R, then pass under road bridge and turn sharply R (Bucharova) at T-junction. Cross Labe and turn L (Ulice Horská), then turn L at T-junction (sp Špindlerův Mlýn, Route 295)

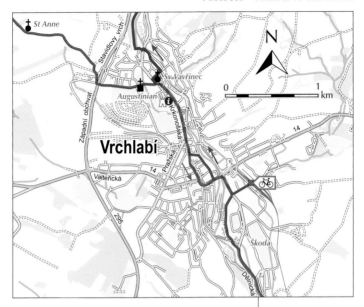

through **Hořejší Vrchlabí** (4km, 516m) (accommodation, refreshments).

Follow Route 295 along Labe valley, ascending steadily through forest passing Herlikovice (accommodation, refreshments) and **Labská** dam R (13.5km, 699m) (accommodation). Continue beside lake R into **Špindlerův Mlýn** (16km, 722m) (accommodation, refreshments, camping, tourist office).

The premier Czech ski resort, **Špindlerův Mlýn** (pop 1400) is surrounded by the high mountains of Krkonoše national park, including Luční hora (1555m) the second highest peak in Czechia. The resort has 25km of downhill piste serviced by 17 lifts and 100km of cross-country ski trails.

Pass bus station R and immediately before main road crosses Labe, fork L (Harrachova). Pass series of hotels

47

From mid-May to mid-November chairlift which carries cycles, operates at 30min intervals 0800–1800.

Gravel track forking L uphill 200m after U Čtyř Pánů provides a short-cut walking route to Pramen Labe. There are cycle racks here made out of carved tree trunks.

and bars L, with Labe R and continue through forest to reach Medvědin *lanovka* (chairlift) bottom station (17km, 745m) Use chairlift to reach **Medvědín** top station (19km, 1233m) (refreshments). ◀

From top chairlift station, bear L under second chairlift (sp central parking Mísečky) and follow rough asphalt road steadily downhill to reach T-junction on apex of hairpin bend. Turn R and ascend round series of hairpins to reach bus turning circle beside **Vrbatova bouda** refuge (23.5km, 1390m) (refreshments). Turn L beside refuge, continuing on asphalt road across gently rolling moorland past picnic area L at U Čtyř Pánů. ◀ Continue

*The Medvědín chairlift takes cyclists and cycles up into the mountains*

downhill to **Labská bouda** refuge (26.5km, 1340m) (accommodation, refreshments) where asphalt surface ends. As cycling is prohibited beyond refuge, bikes must be left here (cycle racks provided) before continuing on foot for 1km along gravel track to reach **Pramen Labe** (Elbe spring) (1386m), 400m before Polish border.

*Labská bouda, 1km from the Elbe spring, is the nearest cycles are allowed*

# STAGE 1

*Elbe Spring to Hostinné*

| | |
|---|---|
| **Start** | Labská bouda (1340m) (1km walk from Elbe spring) |
| **Finish** | Hostinné, Deymova bridge (352m) |
| **Distance** | 40km |
| **Ascent** | 160m |
| **Descent** | 1148m |
| **Waymarking** | none to Vrchlabí, then Czech National Cycle Route 2 to Hostinné |

This stage descends steadily on forest tracks and quiet roads through the thickly forested Krkonoše mountains, past a series of small ski resorts to reach the Labe valley at Vrchlabí. It then continues through a narrow valley to the small industrial town of Hostinné, once a major centre for the production of paper.

The Elbe rises near **Pramen Labe** spring (1386m) in the Krkonoše mountains, close to the border between Poland and Czechia and one of the most popular walking destinations in the country. The ornamental spring and a wall depicting the coats of arms of 26 major cities on the river are between 150m and 300m from the true spring which is in a protected area inaccessible to visitors. Pramen Labe is only accessible on foot.

After visiting **Pramen Labe** (Elbe spring) on foot, return to **Labská bouda** refuge (1340m) (accommodation, refreshments). Cycle on asphalt road bearing R uphill and follow this across rolling open moorland to reach bus-turning circle at **Vrbatova bouda** refuge (3.5km, 1390m) (refreshments). Continue downhill round five hairpins to small ski resort of **Horní Mísečky** (8km, 1036m) (accommodation, refreshments).

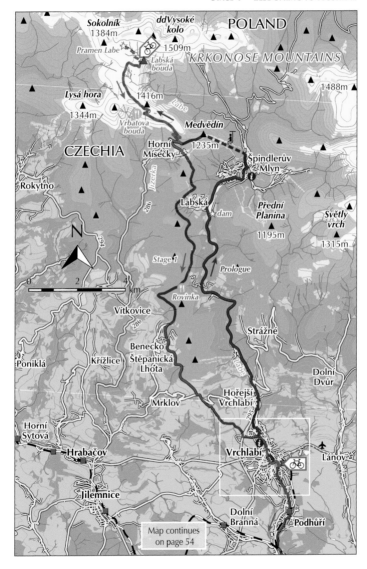

Map continues on page 54

51

Pass bus shelter L then where road bears R, turn L and immediately R on gravel track under chairlift across beginners' ski-run and into forest. Fork R into open area (Stadion) passing Chata Stopa bar R. Follow track ahead through barrier to re-enter forest and continue descending gently, now on asphalt. Pass under chairlift and cross ski piste then ascend slightly, now on gravel track, before descending to reach road at Tridomi hamlet. Bear R and continue on road winding through forest past **Rovinka** (14.5km, 853m) (refreshments). Pass Bellevue hotel R then emerge on main road at apex of hairpin bend. Fork L uphill into upper part of **Benecko** (18km, 866m) (accommodation, refreshments).

Follow road, now downhill, then turn L at T-junction beside sports club car park in Křížovky. After 300m, fork R slightly uphill to reach Kněžice hamlet, then bear R at T-junction. ◀ Continue descending with view of Vrchlabí ahead past **St Anne's** chapel L then bear R at triangular junction and go ahead over small crossroads. Turn L on pedestrian/cyclist bridge over Vrchlabí by-pass. Go ahead (Hřbitovní), passing Vrchlabí Krkonošská museum in old monastery R. Continue on Husova to Náměstí Miru

Ignore no through road sign, this applies only to motor vehicles.

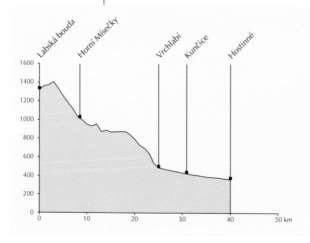

square in **Vrchlabí** (24.5km, (486m) (accommodation, refreshments, camping, tourist office, cycle shop, station).

*Vrchlabí castle was the first Renaissance castle in Bohemia*

**Vrchlabí** (pop 13,000) is the first town on the Elbe. Known in German as Hohenelbe and populated mainly by German Lutherans, it grew from the 15th century as a mining and metal-working centre using power from the fast-flowing Labe. The castle, built (1546) for German industrialist Krystof Gendorf, was the first Renaissance-style palace in Bohemia. After the creation of Czechoslovakia in 1919, many Germans left. All remaining Germans were expelled after the Second World War. Nowadays, the main employer is a Škoda car factory which ironically is owned by Volkswagen, a German car company.

Turn R (Krkonošská) through town centre then go ahead at one-way system (Slovanská). Go ahead over two crossroads and join cycle track L of road. At next crossroads, go ahead onto main road (Tyršova) and follow this bearing L. Cross Labe and turn R at roundabout

(Dělnická, first exit, sp Hostinné). Turn first R (Ulice Žižkova) and pass through industrial area then turn R (rejoining Dělnická using cycle track L) past Škoda car factory L. Where cycle track ends, fork L (Ulice Poštovní). Cross railway and pass **Podhůří** station R (28.5km, 438m) (station).

Turn R at T-junction (Lipová), then L (Ulice Jana Opletala) just before railway crossing. Where road bears R, continue ahead on minor road. Where this bears R, turn L over stream and follow gravel track with wooded hillside rising L. Dog-leg R and L across railway then emerge on road and turn sharply L. Turn L at crossroads, then R at end to reach main road in **Kunčice nad Labem** (31km, 413m) (station).

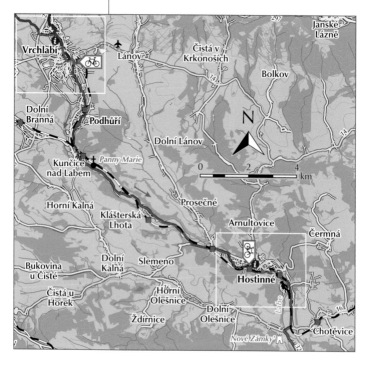

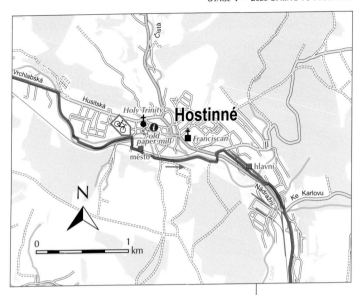

Turn L (sp Hostinné), following main road past Panny Marie (Ascension) chapel L with Labe behind houses and trees R. Continue past KVK stone-works L. ▶ Cross railway and river, then pass through **Klášterská Lhota** (35km, 379m) (station). Cross railway again, then bear L at junction with minor road and cross railway beside Prosečné station R (station). Turn R at T-junction (Vrchlabská, sp Hostinné), then cross Labe on girder bridge and fork immediately R through barriers onto riverside track. Cross covered bridge over millstream then follow track along island between Labe R and millstream L to reach T-junction in **Hostinné** (40km, 352m) (accommodation, refreshments, tourist office, station). ▶

KVK stone-works has the longest industrial cableway in Europe. Now disused, it previously brought architectural limestone 8km from Černy Důl quarries to Kunčice.

For town centre, turn L (Deymova) over millstream then R (Karla Kliče) and second R (Horní Brána) opposite church to reach main square after 300m.

55

## HOSTINNÉ

*The giants on Hostinné town hall were turned to stone for terrorising the town*

The medieval town of Hostinné (pop 4400), first mentioned in 1270, suffered a devastating fire in 1610. The town was subsequently rebuilt around an arcaded main square with a Renaissance-style town hall and Baroque plague column. The town hall façade holds statues of two 5m-tall giants who, according to legend, terrorised the town until they were caught and turned to stone. The Franciscan monastery (1684) fell into disrepair during the Communist era but has recently undergone major restoration and now houses cultural and social centres with a museum and art gallery. It won the Czech restored building of the year award in 2012. In 1835, the ruins of Hostinné castle beside the Labe were converted into the first paper mill in the country. Although it closed in 1985 and is now disused, the buttresses of the old castle are still evident on the rear of the building.

## STAGE 2

*Hostinné to Jaroměř*

| | |
|---|---|
| **Start** | Hostinné, Deymova bridge (352m) |
| **Finish** | Jaroměř, Jaromírova bridge (252m) |
| **Distance** | 35.5km |
| **Ascent** | 144m |
| **Descent** | 244m |
| **Waymarking** | Route 2 |

This stage continues gently descending from the Krkonoše mountains following the Labe valley, though a short ascent is made to Nemojov, 75m above the river. The going is mostly on quiet country roads or dedicated rural cycle paths.

From T-junction on millstream island in **Hostinné**, follow road (Deymova) S over Labe. Continue across railway then turn L (V Lipkách), passing Hostinné město station L. Where road ends at T-junction, continue ahead on cycle track beside Labe L. At end, turn L over Labe then dog-leg L and R across main road into K Čapka. Turn first R (Kaštanová) and continue past Hostinné hlavni station L (refreshments, station) on cycle track beside railway. Where this emerges beside main road, turn L across railway and R along other side then fork R (U Konírny)

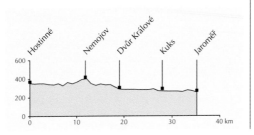

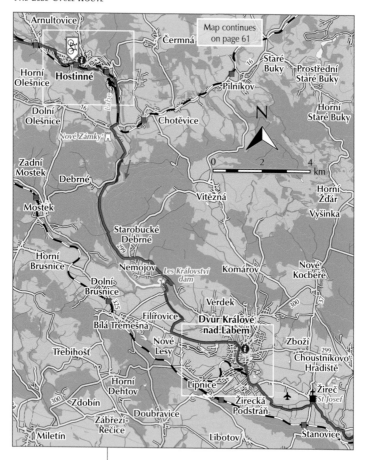

Map continues on page 61

parallel with railway. At end bear R ahead on main road (Nádražní). Follow this to T-junction, then turn R across railway and Labe and turn L (sp Dvůr Králové) in Nové Zámky (4.5km, 345m).

Where road comes close to Labe, turn L over river then R at crossing of tracks, undulating beside river. Emerge on main road (Route 299) in Horní Debrné

(7km, 332m) (accommodation in Debrné, 1km off route) and bear L following main road uphill through forest to reach **Nemojov** (11.5km, 404m) (accommodation, refreshments).

Cycle downhill, then turn R through forest (sp Bílá Třemešná). Bear L over **Les Království** dam (13.5km, 330m) (refreshments). ▶ Bear L and where forest ends after 400m, turn L on quiet road. Keep L at fork and continue downhill on gravel track to road junction by bus shelter in **Filířovice** (15.5km, 334m). Turn R to reach crossroads in **Nové Lesy** (16.5km, 336m) and turn L. Continue downhill past zoo/safari park R, then join cycle track L and follow this (Štefánikova) bearing R beside Labe. Turn L (Husova) over river into **Dvůr Králové nad Labem** (19.5km, 288m) (accommodation, refreshments, camping, tourist office, cycle shop, station).

Turn R at first crossroads (nábřeží Jiřího Wolkera) and continue between sports ground L and Labe R. Where road turns L away from river, continue ahead on gravel

The dam, with its two castellated towers, was built in the early 20th century to control water levels after flooding in 1897. When built it was the largest dam in Czechoslovakia.

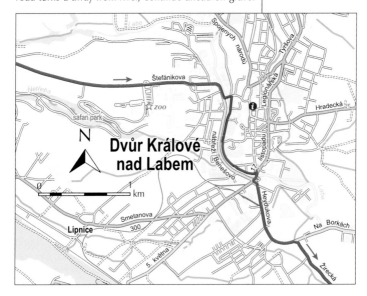

## DVŮR KRÁLOVÉ

The old centre of Dvůr Králové (pop 15,700) is gathered around the arcaded Masaryka Square with the town hall and a Marian column. From 1399 to 1918 it was a dowry town owned by the crown with income from rents and taxes used to fund the household of the queen after the king died. Many dowager queens benefitted from this income but it is thought that only one, Maria Theresia, ever visited the town. In the 19th century, the town became a centre for textile production. The most well-known modern attraction is the zoo and safari park which draws over 500,000 visitors annually. The park specialises in the conservation of African savannah animals and has the biggest collection in Europe, with large and successful breeding herds of zebras, giraffes and buffalos living in open-range drive-through enclosures. Altogether there are more than 2000 animals from 500 species. Their most important achievement is as the only zoo in the world to have bred northern white rhinoceros in captivity.

*Dvůr Králové zoo runs a successful breeding programme for white rhinoceros*

track beside Labe. Keep R at road junction, passing under pipe bridge to continue beside river. At complicated road junction, turn R over Labe to reach roundabout. Bear L (Heydukova, third exit, sp Zirec) and continue under pipe bridge. After second pipe bridge, fork R (Žirecká) and continue out of town into open country. Where surface ahead becomes gravel, turn L (asphalt) past **Žirecká Podstráň** R (22.5km, 284m). Keep L at road junction, then turn L at T-junction into **Žireč** (24.5km, 279m) (refreshments, station).

In 1634, the old Renaissance-style castle at **Žireč** (pop 450) was purchased by the Jesuits who converted it into a Baroque-style convent. After the abolition of the Jesuit order in 1773 it fell into disrepair and in Communist times it was used as a retirement home. In 2001 ownership reverted to a congregation of nuns who have restored the Baroque building which now houses St Josef's Home, a nursing care facility for 88 patients with severe multiple sclerosis. The adjacent St Anna church houses a unique musical instrument, a Baroque bell piano that chimes bells when the keys are played. Originally installed in 1732, it was fully restored in 2010 and can be heard annually on the Saturday nearest the feast of St Anne (26 July).

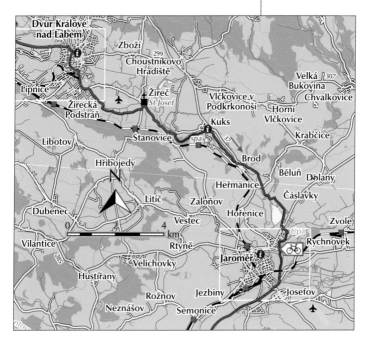

*The mineral water spa at Kuks was one of the most celebrated European spas in the 18th century*

Can be muddy when wet.

At next T-junction, turn sharply R (sp Kuks). After 1.5km, turn L (sp Kuks) and cross Labe to **Stanovice** (26.5km, 273m) (accommodation, refreshments). Turn R beside river and where road ends continue ahead through barrier on unsurfaced track with Labe R. ◄ Emerge on road and bear R into **Kuks** (28km, 268m) (accommodation, refreshments, tourist office, station).

In 1692, three mineral water springs near **Kuks** (pop 260) were combined into a small spa. When experts from Baden-Baden confirmed the healing effects of the water, the facilities were expanded from 1707 including an octagonal church, hospital, theatre, pharmacy and other buildings all in Baroque style. Interiors and exteriors were decorated with sculptures by Matthias Braun. For a few years it was one of the most celebrated spas in Europe until a flood in 1740 destroyed much of the infrastructure and put it out of business. The hospital, church and pharmacy have been restored and can be visited.

Special measures have been taken to preserve the outdoor statuary and prevent further decay.

Pass bridge leading R over Labe to **Kuks** spa complex and climb steeply on cobbled road. Bear R at road junction, then fork R downhill on asphalt track out of village. Continue on cycle track beside Labe, then pass under two road bridges to reach T-junction in **Brod** (30.5km, 263m) (refreshments). Turn R through village, then where road ends continue ahead on track to cross road at **Heřmanice** (32km, 262m) (refreshments). Follow asphalt cycle track ahead, winding through fields to reach T-junction beside crematorium. Turn R, then after 650m, fork R. Turn third L, passing under main road, then bear R beside road. After 100m, turn sharply L and follow cycle track to reach Labe. Continue beside river, then emerge on road and turn L (Na Úpě) to reach triangular junction with main road in **Jaroměř** (35.5km, 252m) (accommodation, refreshments, tourist office, station). ▶

To reach town centre turn R on main road (Jaromírova) for 850m.

*The main square in Jaroměř*

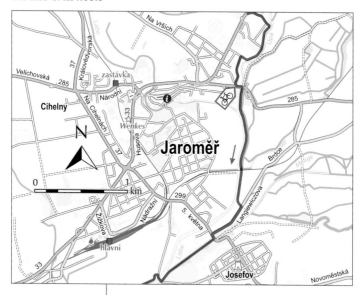

**Jaroměř** (pop 12,400) has a small medieval core with a main square on the site of an ancient castle, of which only one gate and a bell tower remain. The arcaded square has a Marian column and many old buildings. In the 19th century the town became a railway junction town and there is a small railway museum in an old railway depot. Wenkes department store, which nowadays hosts the town museum, is an early example of Modernist architecture designed in 1910 by Josef Gočár. When German Nazis occupied part of the country (1938), Jaroměř became the border town between German-occupied Sudetenland and nominally independent Czechoslovakia.

# STAGE 3
## *Jaroměř to Pardubice*

| | |
|---|---|
| **Start** | Jaroměř, Jaromírova bridge (252m) |
| **Finish** | Pardubice, Zámecká St (220m) |
| **Distance** | 46km |
| **Waymarking** | Route 2 |

This stage first follows riverside cycle tracks from Jaroměř through Hradec Králové to Vysoká then a main road to Pardubice. Gently descending throughout.

From T-junction with Na Úpě in **Jaroměř**, turn L (Jaromírova) over river Upa and immediately R on cycle track beside river. Pass confluence with Labe and continue under railway bridge. Emerge on main road and turn R (Langiewiczova) to reach T-junction. Turn L (5. května) on cobbled bridge over river Metuje (2km, 254m) and immediately R on cycle track beside river, with **Josefov** fortress (accommodation, refreshments) on hillcrest above L.

> **Josefov fortress** was built (1780–1787) to defend the newly defined northern border of the Habsburg empire against Prussia after the end of the Seven Years' War. Named after Emperor Josef II, its design was influenced by the works of French military engineer Vauban. The fortress is surrounded by bastions, ravelins and moats, with 42km of underground corridors, some of which can be visited. Inside the walls are extensive barracks and civilian buildings. For 80 years it faced no military threat, being used for much of that time to incarcerate foreign prisoners of war and internal political prisoners. By 1866 its technology was already outdated

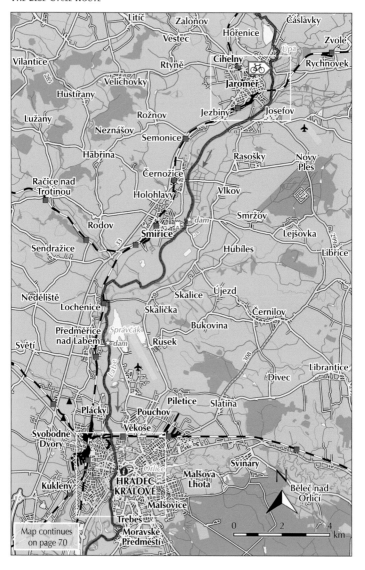

Map continues
on page 70

when an invading Prussian army simply by-passed Josefov on their way to confront the Austrian army near Hradec Králové. Since then it has been used as a barracks, command centre and training camp. From 1968 to 1991 it was occupied by Soviet Russian troops before ending its military role in the 1990s. Some restoration has been undertaken, but much remains to be done.

After passing below fortress bastions, turn R across Labe just downstream of its confluence with river Metuje. Turn L to circle old steam pumping station and join riverside track, now on opposite bank. Keep L at fork beside sewage works to continue beside river. In **Černožice** (6.5km, 250m) (refreshments, station), go ahead over bridge approach road and continue along riverside track to reach road turning circle in **Smiřice** (9km, 243m) (refreshments, station).

The Baroque chateau, farm and attached chapel of the Apparition at **Smiřice** (pop 2900) were built in the late 17th century. For most of the 18th and 19th centuries it was owned by the Austrian emperor and used as administrative quarters for the imperial estates, before ownership passed to the Czechoslovak state in 1918. After various usages, including as a brewery, it was sold to Belgian owners in 2013 and is undergoing renovation.

Turn L (Ant Seligera), then bear R and fork L (U Stadionu). Go ahead over main road then fork L and turn R to continue along riverside track, passing chateau R. At end of village, follow track bearing R away from Labe, then turn sharply L to return to riverside. After 3km, follow track away from river, winding through fields, then after further 1.5km, turn L and fork L to cross railway and reach road in **Lochenice** (15km, 239m) (refreshments, station).

Turn L, then recross railway beside station R. Just before road crosses Labe, turn R beside river and follow this to reach road beside dam at **Předměřice nad Labem** (17km, 239m) (refreshments, station).

Turn L across dam, then immediately R on cycle track along opposite side of river. Where track divides, continue on track nearest to river to reach road and turn R over Labe into **Plácky** (20.5km, 233m) (refreshments). Turn L on opposite bank along riverside cycle track and follow this under railway and two road bridges into **Hradec Králové** (22.5km, 233m) (accommodation, refreshments, tourist office, cycle shop, station).

Immediately after second bridge, bear R onto cycle track with car parking spaces R. Where parking spaces end, turn R across road and follow dual-use cycle track as it circles nám Svobody square anti-clockwise. ◀ Cross three roads radiating from Labe bridge, then pass university (between third and fourth roads) and turn R on cycle track between trees to continue following Labe. Pass art nouveau-style hydroelectric power station L, then just before motorway bridge, fork R up to

To reach city centre, turn L across Labe bridge.

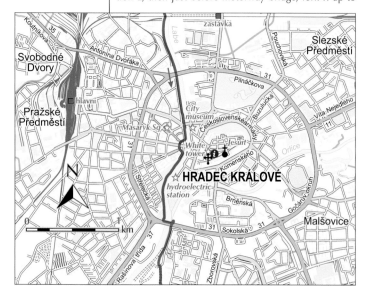

## HRADEC KRÁLOVÉ

Art nouveau-style hydroelectric power station in Hradec Králové

The long history of Hradec Králové (pop 93,000) (charter granted 1225) is reflected in a wide variety of architectural styles. The oldest building, the Gothic cathedral of St Spirit on Velké nám (Great Sq) is surrounded by 16th-century Renaissance buildings including the White tower and old town hall. These were joined in the 17th century by a Baroque-style Jesuit church and college. In 1765 the city was encircled by extensive defensive fortifications intended to defend Austria against Prussian advances and a once-attractive city took on the dour appearance of a military fort. These fortifications proved useless in 1866, when a Prussian attack at the Battle of Königgrätz (the German name for Hradec Králové) fought in open country 12km north west of the city, resulted in an overwhelming victory for Prussia. Subsequently the fortifications were demolished and an international competition was held for a new urban plan. Work started before the First World War, under the influence of Jan Kotěra (regarded as the founder of Czech Modernism and himself influenced by the Viennese Secession movement), then continued in the 1920s and 30s led by Josef Gočár. The result was an attractive city with roads radiating from the old city centre, intersected by an orbital network rather like a spider's web. Many Modernist structures still stand, including the city museum (Kotěra, 1912) and Masaryk Square (Gočár, 1926).

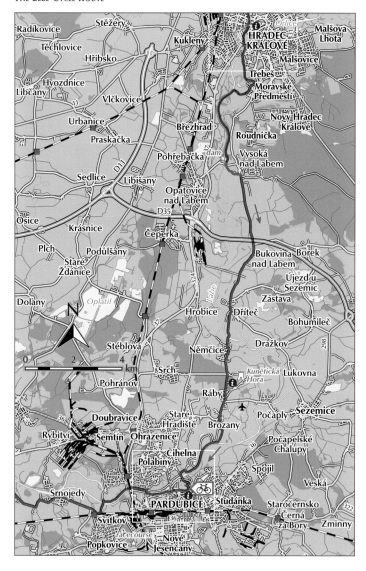

bridge and turn L over Labe using cycle track L. At end of bridge, turn L down to riverbank and sharply L back under bridge. Follow riverside track, soon bearing L away from river. Dog-leg L and R through allotments, then follow track under pipe bridge to reach road head in **Moravské Předměstí** (25.5km, 230m) (accommodation, refreshments).

Continue ahead (Machkova), then turn R (K Labi) at triangular junction opposite house 32. Where road turns L opposite house 16 continue ahead and, after 100m bear R onto riverside cycle track. Follow river R and pass Opatovice dam (30km, 227m). ▸ Go ahead over crossroads and follow track winding through fields. Pass sports club L and bear R on road. Fork first R and at end turn R on main road in **Vysoká nad Labem** (31.5km, 234m) (accommodation, refreshments). Cross motorway and continue to **Bukovina nad Labem** (34.5km, 240m). Pass under railway to reach **Dříteč** (36km, 226m) (refreshments).

*Kunětická Hora castle was built in the 15th century on a low volcanic hill*

Opatovice dam was built in 1513 to supply water for the 35km-long Opatovice canal, which formerly allowed small boats to reach Hradec Králové.

Heavily fortified 15th-century Kunětická Hora castle stands on a low volcanic hill 500m from the route. It is a national monument and can be visited.

Soon after joining Labe, 969km post on opposite bank shows navigable river distance from Cuxhaven.

Fork R in village, following main road over Labe. Continue through **Němčice** (39km, 226m) then keep L at fork. Continue past entrance to Kunětická Hora castle L (accommodation, refreshments, tourist office). ◄ Follow road through **Ráby** (41km, 220m) (refreshments, cycle shop) then join cycle track L and continue to **Brozany** (41.5km, 220m) (refreshments).

Fork L opposite house 29, then at end of built-up area, go ahead on middle of three tracks to cycle along flood dyke. Continue to reach Labe and turn R beside river L. ◄ Cycle past swimming pool complex R, then bear L (Kunětická) and turn L over Labedam. Dog-leg L and R to join cycle track through trees, with white walls of Pardubice zámek castle R. Follow track bearing R around castle, then turn L opposite castle entrance (Příhrádek, cobbles). Pass under gate tower, then bear R (Zámecká) through arch. Stage ends at small arch on R between building numbers 17 and 16 in **Pardubice** (46km, 220m) (accommodation, refreshments, camping, tourist office, cycle shop, station).

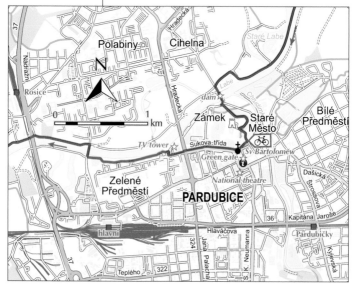

## PARDUBICE

Pardubice (pop 90,000), which nowadays is the highest point of navigation on the Labe, was a medieval city with a heyday in the early 16th century when the Pernštýn family were in control. They developed the castle as a four-winged Renaissance palace and, after a fire in 1538 had destroyed the old town, oversaw the rebuilding of Stare Město with a Renaissance main square, overlooked by the Green gate, surrounded by attractive streets. After the Pernštýns suffered financial problems (1560), the city was forfeited to the emperor and remained under imperial control for 300 years during which period the city's economy stagnated, with the castle being used for commercial rather than residential purposes. The coming of the railways after 1845 brought industrial growth, particularly of chemical and food industries. In 1863 the castle was bought by private owners and remained in private hands until taken over by the Communist government in 1952. After this it was neglected and part of the ceilings collapsed in 1977. Restoration began in 1994 and it now hosts an art gallery and a museum. Strong industrial development started after 1919, mainly of chemical and electrical companies. Rapid development after 1948 saw the construction of big new state housing projects and state-owned factories. Chemical and electrical production remain important industries.

In sporting circles, the Grand Pardubice steeplechase, held on the second Sunday in October, is regarded as the toughest horse race in the world. First raced in 1874, the modern cross-country course is 6900m long with 31 varied and challenging jumps. Accidents and injuries to both horses and jockeys are common. In 1909 no horses finished while in 1920 there was no approved winner as the only finisher was outside the time limit!

# STAGE 4
## Pardubice to Kolín

| | |
|---|---|
| **Start** | Pardubice, Zámecká St (220m) |
| **Finish** | Kolín, Jiráskovo Sq (197m) |
| **Distance** | 52km |
| **Waymarking** | Route 2 |

Two small rises (40m each) are crossed as the route continues to follow the Labe on a mixture of quiet country roads, field paths and riverside tracks. Some of these tracks are unsurfaced and can prove difficult after rain. A series of small villages are passed, though the only intermediate accommodation is at Týnec nad Labem after 38km.

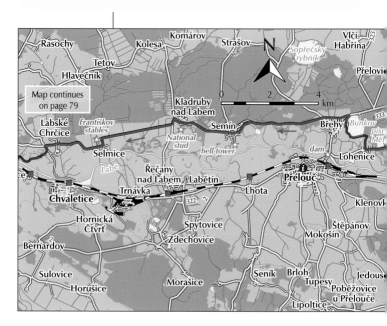

Map continues on page 79

From Zamecká in **Pardubice**, cycle SW under arch between buildings 17 and 16 following Kostelní. Pass Sv Bartoloměj church L and continue on cycle track beside dual carriageway Sukova Třida. Go ahead over traffic lights, then turn R at roundabout. After 40m, turn L and fork R to join cycle track beside Labe R and follow this past series of high-rise apartment buildings. Fork R by last building and turn R over Labe using cycle track R. Turn L immediately after bridge on cycle track along opposite bank. Pass under road and rail bridges and continue out of city. At next bridge, follow track R away from river and turn R over bridge. On opposite bank, join cycle track R of road and follow this bearing R past **Svitkov** station (accommodation, station). After village cycle track crosses to L and continues to **Srnojedy** (6.5km, 217m).

Where cycle track ends, join road and follow this winding through village to **Lány na Důlku** (9km, 220m). Where main road forks L beside wayside cross, go

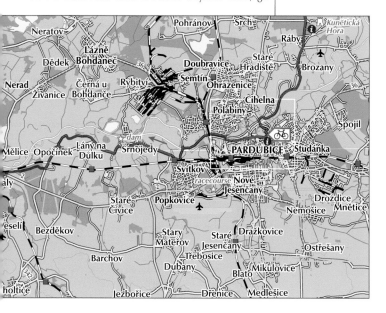

straight ahead on road between houses, ascending gently. Where village ends continue on gravel track, eventually descending steeply to join road. Bear L, ascending into **Opočínek** (11.5km, 218m) (station) and turn sharply R immediately before small ochre-coloured bell tower. At end of village turn R at T-junction to regain main road. Cross railway bridge and turn R on rough gravel track into forest. Descend on unsurfaced track to emerge beside main road and bear R into **Valy** (14.5km, 216m) (refreshments, station).

In centre of village, turn R, then pass under railway and over Labe. Continue ahead through **Mělice** (15km, 215m) then pass Mělice recreation area (refreshments, camping) in old aggregate pits R to reach **Lohenice** (17km, 213m) (refreshments). Turn R opposite house 61, then at beginning of forest turn L at five-way track junction. Follow unsurfaced track along shore of Buňkov lake R, then bear L away from lake and turn R past campsite R. Turn R at T-junction and after 250m turn L (Na Hrázi) past **Břehy** (19.5km, 213m) (refreshments, camping, tourist office – in Přelouč 3km off route). At end of village, go ahead across main road and continue through forest to **Semín** (24.5km, 211m) (refreshments, camping). ◄ Continue ahead to reach **Kladruby nad Labem** (27km, 209m) (refreshments).

Semín church has a free-standing 16th-century wooden bell tower. The chateau was the birthplace of architect Josef Gočár (1880–1945).

The castle at Kladruby nad Labem (pop 650) houses the **Národní hřebčín Kladruby** (Czech national stud farm). As one of the oldest stud farms in Europe, Kladruby formerly bred horses for the imperial courts in Prague and Vienna. Nowadays they specialise in maintaining the blood line of Starokladrubský horses, the oldest breed in the country. About 250 horses are bred annually. They are born black but become white as they age, being fully white by 10 years old. Although there are no longer royal duties for the horses in Czechia, horses are supplied to royal courts in Denmark and Sweden and can be seen pulling carriages on the streets of Copenhagen and Stockholm. In Czechia

they are used as police horses and sold to private individuals for leisure riding. The castle, stud farm and adjoining carriage museum can be visited on a guided tour (tours run hourly on the hour from 1000–1600, April–October).

Pass castle, stud farm and lookout tower (former water tower) L, then turn L (sp Týnec nad Labem). Opposite rear entrance to castle, turn R (sp Týnec nad Labem) and continue straight ahead on avenue through fields of horses to Františkov stables. ▸ Turn L in front of stables and after 300m, turn R before village of **Selmice** (31km, 204m) (refreshments). Continue winding through fields and forest to **Labské Chrčice** (33km, 205m).

Cycle through village then turn L between last building L and village pond R. After 150m, fork R on unsurfaced track and follow this, winding through low-lying marshland of Týnecké mokřiny to reach Labe. ▸ Turn R along riverbank and continue to tennis club. Bear R away from river then fork L onto road head. Follow road (Mannova) ascending steeply and bearing R to reach

*Kladruby nad Labem castle houses the Czech national stud farm*

Františkov, part of the national stud, is used to stable foals and young horses under three years old.

Track can be muddy when wet.

77

*The ruined castle in Týnec nad Labem*

Masarykovo nám Square in centre of **Týnec nad Labem** (38km, 237m) (accommodation, refreshments, camping, tourist office, station).

**Týnec nad Labem** (pop 2000) sits atop a small hill overlooking the Labe. In the centre, Masarykovo nám Square, has a Marian column and some attractive buildings including the old post office. General Melas (1729–1806), the leader of the Austrian army during the Napoleonic Wars, is buried here. After a series of victories, his army was decisively defeated by Napoleon at the Battle of Marengo (1800), where he was injured and subsequently retired. His name

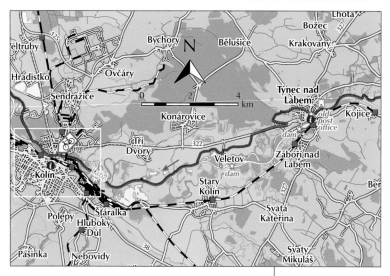

lives on in the oratorio to Puccini's opera *Tosca*, where he is mentioned in relation to Marengo.

Cross square and continue ahead (Krále Jiřiho), then fork L beside house 392. Descend, going ahead past pizzeria L then fork L under power line on unsurfaced track. Fork L on track between field L and forest R and follow this curving L uphill. At end, bear L on road along top of ridge into **Lžovice** (40.5km, 238m) (refreshments). Turn R downhill opposite house 52, then R again onto main road, continuing downhill into open country. After 1.5km, turn L on unsurfaced track and follow this through fields, forking R to reach staggered junction. ▸ Continue ahead past pumping station L and follow rough asphalt track to T-junction, then turn L into **Veletov** (44km, 200m).

Turn R at crossroads in centre of village and continue out of village. Fork L at track junction, then follow track past aggregates quarry R to reach Labe. Turn R beside river and follow riverside track for 6km. Every time this

Track can be muddy when wet.

79

The city centre is on the opposite bank. To reach it, continue ahead to roundabout and turn L over the Labe on Starý most bridge.

bears R away from river, fork L to continue along river-bank. Go under railway bridge and pass power station R. Turn R away from river on track beneath road bridge, then turn L (Tovární) to reach crossroads at Jiráskovo nám Square in **Kolín** (52km, 197m) (accommodation, refreshments, tourist office, cycle shop, station). ◄

**Kolín** (pop 31,000) was founded in the 13th century and surrounded by double walls, a few bastions from which still survive. The most notable buildings, Sv Bartoloměj cathedral in Gothic style and the neighbouring lookout tower, stand on a ridge just above the old centre. Other important buildings can be found in Karlovo nám Square. From the 15th century until the Second World War, Kolín had a large Jewish community that lived in a ghetto west of the town centre. Here there is a synagogue and the second largest Jewish cemetery in Bohemia.

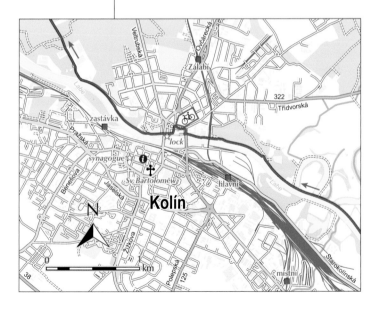

# STAGE 5
*Kolín to Nymburk*

| | |
|---|---|
| **Start** | Kolín, Jiráskovo Square (197m) |
| **Finish** | Nymburk, Na Fortně (189m) |
| **Distance** | 27.5km |
| **Waymarking** | Route 2 |

This almost completely flat stage follows the riverside cycle track as the Labe meanders through forest from Kolín to Nymburk. From Kolín going is mostly on unsurfaced or gravel paths but after Osada Labe, good quality asphalt extends through Nymburk.

From Jiráskovo nám in **Kolín**, follow Mlýnská S to reach Labe and turn R beside Kolín lock. Go under road bridge, then fork L onto riverside cycle track. Pass under pedestrian bridge then fork L to continue along riverbank. Beside sports complex R, fork R away from river (Brankovická, sp ZKO Kolín-Borky). Cycle through forest and pass sewage works R. At three-way split of tracks, take middle track into forest and continue to reach riverbank. Pass Klavarský lock and fork L to continue beside river on concrete block track. This becomes unsurfaced and turns sharply L. Follow unsurfaced riverside track for 3.25km to reach T-junction at Osada Labe hamlet (8.5km, 190m). ▶ Turn R away from river on asphalt road to reach triangular junction. Fork L (Ulice Máčidla) through **Velký Osek** (10.5km, 194m) (accommodation, refreshments, station). Turn R at T-junction to reach main road, then turn L (Revoluční), joining cycle lane R and cycle through village. Where buildings end, fork R onto cycle track. Pass under motorway, and fork R away from road. Turn R at T-junction, then bear L (sp Libice N Cidl) and cross river Cidlina into **Libice nad Cidlinou** (14km, 189m) (refreshments, station).

Unsurfaced track becomes muddy when wet.

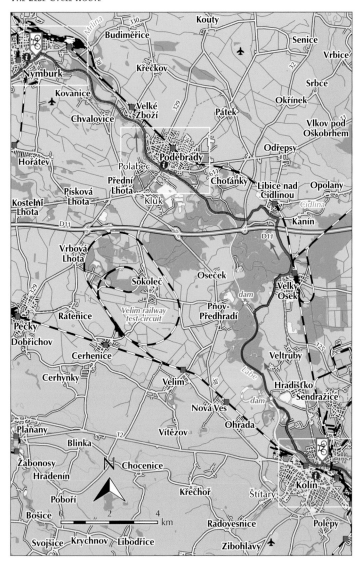

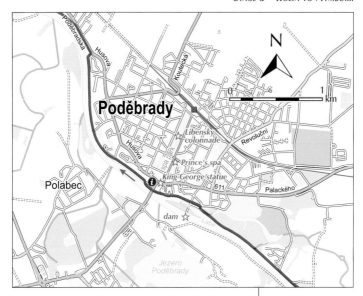

Immediately after bridge, fork L on narrow road (Jižní) along edge of village. Where houses end, turn L on tree-lined track through fields. Pass under bridge, then follow track beside Cidlina to reach confluence with Labe (refreshments, camping at Cidlina). Continue beside river to reach **Poděbrady** lock (19km, 188m) (accommodation, refreshments, tourist office, cycle shop, station).

## PODĚBRADY

Poděbrady (pop 14000) has two distinct elements, the castle district, a 14th- to 15th-century old town around the riverside castle, and an early 20th century spa park, which runs north from the castle district as far as the station. The old town was favoured by King George (ruled 1458–1471) who was born here and has a statue in Jiřiho nám Square. The old castle has been rebuilt several times; the current Baroque style dates from 1724. Nearby, the old town hall is a Renaissance building while the new town hall

*The Libensky colonnade in the spa park at Poděbrady*

is neo-Renaissance style (1907). In 1905, when drilling a new well for the castle, an iron-rich mineral spring was tapped. The water was found to have health benefits and other shafts were drilled. By 1930 there were 16 active mineral springs. The first baths were opened in 1908 and the spa park was developed by architect František Janda in art nouveau style. Important buildings include the Libensky colonnade and the Prince's spa. The spa park has recently been extensively renovated.

Just before lock, dog-leg R and L over side-stream then continue beside Labe past castle R and go under bridge. After 1.5km, bear L beside main road then after 200m, bear L to rejoin riverside track in **Velké Zboží** (22km, 185m) (station). At end of built-up area, continue under road bridge following riverside track to reach Nymburk dam. Bear R opposite hydroelectric power station, crossing river Mrlina, then fork L on asphalt road between arms of old city moat. Bear L, with city walls R and waterfront L, to reach triangular road junction with Na Fortně in **Nymburk** (27.5km, 189m) (accommodation, refreshments, tourist office, cycle shop, station).

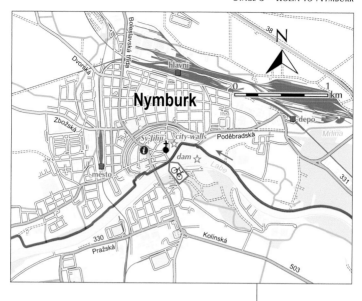

*The city walls at Nymburk originally overlooked two moats*

**Nymburk** (pop 15,000) was a 13th-century walled town beside the Labe with two protective moats fed by the river. The walls were made of brick with 50 towers and five gates, one of which opened directly onto a bridge over the Labe. Both of the moats and part of the walls remain. Inside the walls the most significant buildings are the Renaissance old town hall on nám Přemyslovců and brick-built Sv Jiliji church, in north German Gothic style. Industrialisation arrived in the 19th century and Nymburk became an important railway junction town with railway workshops, depots and marshalling yards. A railway colony garden village was built for railway workers. Some of the colony buildings survive, though most were demolished during the Communist era and replaced with tower blocks.

# STAGE 6
*Nymburk to Prague*

| | |
|---|---|
| **Start** | Nymburk, Na Fortně (189m) |
| **Finish** | Libeň (Prague 8), Rokytka weir (185m) |
| **Distance** | 54.5km |
| **Ascent** | 126m |
| **Descent** | 130m |
| **Waymarking** | Route 2 (Nymburk– Lázně Toušeň), Route 17 (Lázně Toušeň–Horni Počernice), Route A26 (Horni Počernice–Prague (Libeň). |

The first half of this stage, as far as Lazné Toušeň, continues following the Labe riverside cycle track much of which is unsurfaced. It then leaves the river and turns south west, climbing over a low ridge before descending through extensive Prague suburbs to reach the river Vlatava. An excursion at the end follows the river into the city centre.

From road junction by riverside in **Nymburk**, cycle SW on riverside track. Pass under road bridge then turn R through car park and immediately L on cycle track (Na Parkáně). Cross bridge over defensive moat, then bear L to reach Labe and turn R on riverside track. Pass under railway bridge and after 1.2km, follow track away from river through scrubland. Bear L, then R beside factory complex to reach road in **Drahelice** (2.5km, 185m) (refreshments).

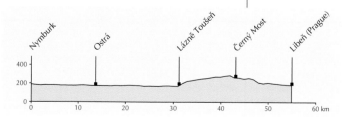

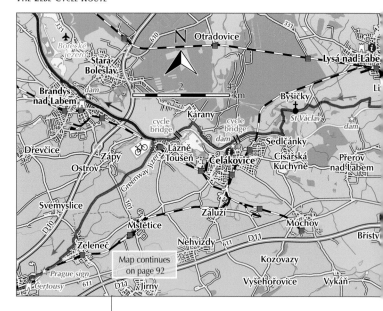

Turn L past factory, then second L on track back to river. Continue on riverside track which soon becomes unsurfaced. Just before lock, bear R away from river to reach road in **Kostomlátky** (5km, 183m). Turn L (5 Května) and follow road winding through village, then turn L between houses 45 and 44, following track that bears R back to river. Pass **Doubrava** R (7.5km, 179m) and continue to emerge on road just before Hradištko lock (9km, 179m). Fork R beside blue gates on unsurfaced track passing behind lock cottages, then rejoin riverside track and continue past Mydlovarsky luh wetland forest R. Cross narrow bridge over Farsky potok stream to reach weekend home development. Walk your cycle over narrow metal bridge with only one handrail. At 'no through road' sign, turn R away from river to reach Jezero Ostrá lake and circle this anticlockwise to reach road in **Ostrá** (14km, 178m) (refreshments, camping). ◄

Botanicus gardens in Ostra produce organic ingredients from herbs, fruit and vegetables for use in cosmetics.

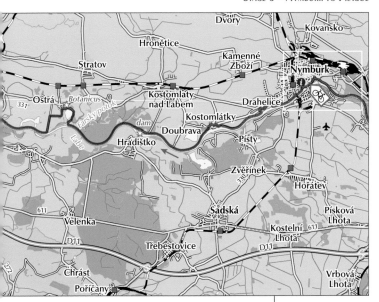

*It is safer to walk over the narrow cycle track bridge across Farsky potok stream*

Turn L beside Botanicus visitor car park, then fork R to follow rough track winding through fields. Turn L at road crossing to reach Labe and bear R on riverside track. Pass weekend homes at Felinka R and more weekend homes at Doubka. Pass under road bridge and immediately after bridge fork L to continue on unsurfaced riverside track which can be muddy when wet. Pass **Litol** R, forking L to follow Labe. Beside pumping station, follow track bearing R away from river, then turn L at crossing of tracks. ◄ Continue on unsurfaced track through fields, forking R at two unwaymarked junctions then go ahead through woods and cross road at Osada Řehačka. Bear R beside woodland and turn L at T-junction to cycle through **Byšičky** (22.5km, 177m).

Pass tiny St Vaclav chapel in middle of roundabout and go ahead on track between houses 6 and 7. Continue beside old arm of Labe L then bear L, winding through forest and fields. Fork R to reach Labe and turn sharply R on track beside river. Pass under railway bridge then emerge on road and follow this under cable-stayed pedestrian/cyclist bridge. ◄ Continue past **Čelákovice** dam (27km, 171m) and follow road (K Přivozu) bearing R away from river into **Kárany** (28.5km, 176m).

Turn L at crossroads (Václavská) then turn R (U Vodárny). Where this ends, turn L (Hlavní) returning to riverbank. Follow riverside track to reach pedestrian/cyclist bridge, then turn R and curve back L to cross bridge over Labe. At end of bridge, turn sharply R to reach riverbank and turn L (Na Nábřeží). Pass **Lázně Toušeň** (refreshments, station) and continue along riverbank to reach road junction at far end of village (31.5km, 171m), where you have a choice of routes. ◄

Turn L (Na Krétě) to reach T-junction with main road. Turn L (Hlavní), then R (Pražská) across railway. Continue ahead onto cycle track ascending steadily through fields and across main road to **Zeleneč** (37km, 256m) (refreshments, station). Bear L on road (Čsl Armády), then turn R beside house 53/71. Follow cycle track behind houses L around edge of village, twice bearing R to keep out of village. At end, bear R on cycle track beside road,

To visit Lysa nad Labem (2km off-route) (accommodation, refreshments, tourist office, station) go straight ahead at road junction.

To visit Čelákovice (accommodation, refreshments, tourist office, cycle shop, station) turn R and L to cross the Labe on the pedestrian/cyclist bridge.

Main route leaves the Labe and continues to Prague following waymarked Greenway Jizera (Route 17). Alternative route (described in Stage 7A) follows the Labe to Mělnik, by-passing Prague.

*A cycle bridge takes the route over the Labe between Kárany and Lázně Toušeň*

continuing to ascend gently. Pass communications mast R and soon reach road sign showing beginning of Praha (Prague) (39km, 260m). ▶

Fork R (no entry, cyclists permitted) then dog-leg L and R (Na Staré Silnici). At T-junction, turn L (Cirkusová), then just before next T-junction, turn L on cycle track under railway. Emerge on road (Vidonická) and after 50m turn sharply R, then go ahead over crossroads (Otovická) into **Horni Počernice** Prague 20 (41.5km, 285m) (accommodation, refreshments, station).

At end, turn L (Jívanská), cross main road and turn R (Mezilesí). At end, bear R ahead past apartment buildings L, then dog-leg R and L over main road onto Šplechnerova, descending steeply. At crossroads, turn R and immediately L on cycle track and continue to reach main road. Turn L on cycle track beside road, passing petrol station L, then bear L and follow cycle track under three bridges of motorway junction. After third bridge, continue ahead over two light-controlled crossings, then go over third crossing and join road ahead between McDonalds R and Centrum **Černý Most** shopping centre L (44km, 254m) (accommodation, refreshments). Where road turns sharply L, continue ahead past end of

For next 20km, route follows waymarked cycle Route A26 through city streets and dedicated cycle tracks to reach Prague city Centrum.

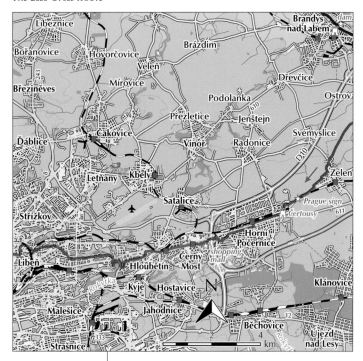

For route through Prague
see more detailed map
opposite

shopping centre and follow cycle track past Černý Most
metro station R. Pass under walkway and dog-leg R and
L beside station. At end of station, bear R and use ramp
to reach upper level. At top, turn sharply L on causeway
above metro tunnel. Follow this for 1km, and where track
divides, fork R to reach Rajská zahrada station.

Bear R to pass front of station, then continue beside
motorway. Bear L to cross side road at traffic lights
then bear R to continue beside motorway. Pass under
bridge then follow slip road away from motorway. Turn
L between apartment blocks and continue over crossroads (Rochovská) in Lehovec (46.5km, 245m) (cycle
shop). At end, dog-leg L and R onto cycle track under
road bridge and continue ahead (V Chaloupkách). Go

ahead (Vaňkova), passing car park R and continue into Šestajovická. At end, turn L (Hloubětínská) and after 250m, turn R on cycle track downhill between gates. Bear R beside sound-proofing fence for motorway, then fork R on gravel track and turn L under motorway in **Hloubětín** (47km, 219m) (accommodation, refreshments).

Dog-leg L and R over river Rokytka then bear R through barrier to reach road. Turn R, then pass under road bridge and turn L at T-junction (Nadernlejnská). Where road bears R, turn L and immediately L again on cycle track, then follow this over motorway bridge. Pass long line of new apartment buildings L and cross road bridge In **Vysočany** Prague 9 (51.5km, 195m) (accommodation, cycle shop, station). Turn R, past Rezidence Eliška modern high-rise building, then follow cycle track over road bridge and continue beside Rokytka R. Cross road beside small bridge and continue on gravel track beside river. Dog-leg L and R across road with tram tracks in centre and continue on cycle track through parkland. Cross next road then at end turn L (Nad Kolčavkou) and immediately fork R. Dog-leg L and R to pass under motorway bridge. At end, turn L up ramp and at top turn sharply

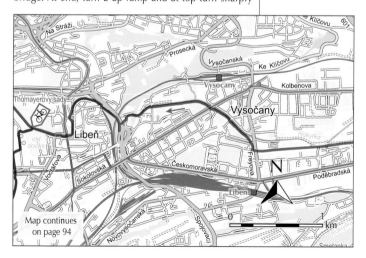

Map continues on page 94

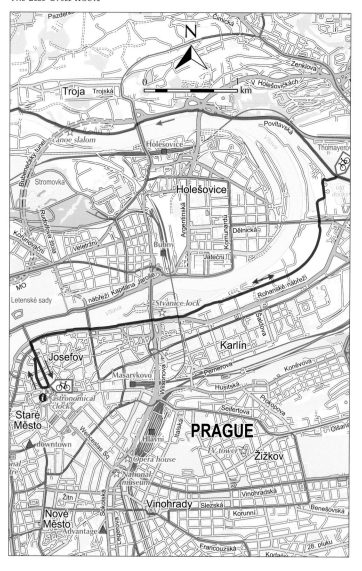

L beside motorway. Pass under railway bridge and follow cycle track bearing L beside Rokytka. Dog-leg R and L over river and continue on opposite bank. Emerge on road (U Rokytky), then cross small square and continue beside river. Continue ahead over crossroads then, where road bears L, continue ahead (U Českvch Loděnic) to reach junction of tracks beside flood barrier pillars where Rokytka reaches river Vltava in **Libeň** Prague 8 (54.5km, 185m) (accommodation, cycle shop). ▸

Here there is a choice of routes. To avoid Prague city centre and continue on Stage 7, cycle ahead beside canal. To visit Prague, turn L and follow excursion route below.

**Excursion to Prague city centre**

Turn L over Rokytka and bear R uphill over former entrance to Prague docks. Bear L to reach road (Menclova) and after 150m turn R on cycle track. Continue under road bridge, then on gravel track across scrubland, eventually emerging beside river Vltava. Pass under three bridges, then fork L up cobbled ramp. At top, beside clocktower, bear L onto main road and continue to reach Čechův most bridge. Turn L opposite bridge passing Právnická fakulta tram station, then where tram tracks turn R continue ahead (Pařížská) through **Josefov** (former Jewish ghetto) to reach Staroměstské nám (Old Town Sq) in centre of **Prague** (5km, 191m) (accommodation, refreshments, youth hostel, tourist office, cycle shop, station).

## PRAGUE

Prague (pop 1,300,000) is the capital city of Czechia. A settlement by a crossing point of the river Vltava was transformed by King Charles IV (ruled 1346–1378) into a capital city for Bohemia. He commissioned the Charles bridge, nowadays one of the most photographed bridges in the world, which for 500 years was the only bridge over the Vltava. On a hilltop west of the river in an area now called Hradčany (castle district), he built a royal castle complex that still has a governing role today as the residence and offices of the Czech president. Here too are St Vitus cathedral and the windows from which 'heretics' were 'defenestrated' during the 15th-century struggles for religious supremacy between Protestant Hussites and Catholics. On the

*Installed in 1410, Prague's astronomical clock is the oldest still operating in the world*

slopes between castle and river, Malá Strana (little quarter) is an area of cobbled streets, noble palaces (many now used as embassies) and walled gardens.

East of the Vltava, Staré Město (old town) is the bustling hub of the city. Here can be found medieval buildings around Staroměstské nám (Old Town Sq) together with 17th-century Baroque buildings. Just north of old town, Josefov was the former Jewish ghetto from which most of the residents were taken by German Nazis to be killed in concentration camps. Poignant remains of synagogues and cemeteries recall this horror while other buildings recall the life of Franz Kafka who grew up here. South of old town, Nové Město (new town) is centred around Véclavské nám (Wenceslas Sq) with buildings including the national theatre and national museum that reflect the growth of 19th-century Czech nationalism and memorials to the struggle against Soviet Communism between 1968 and 1989.

Outside the central city, late 19th- to early 20th-century Prague is an area of low-rise residential buildings and industrial development, well supplied with green parks and gardens. Further out, reaching onto the hills that surround the city, is a post-1945 landscape of Communist-era high-rise apartment buildings and major industrial complexes. However, Prague has put the Communist period well behind it. Many city centre buildings have been renovated, catching up with 50 years of neglect and the city is now one of the most popular tourist destinations in Europe. In the suburbs, many residential flats have been sold to their inhabitants and improved.

# STAGE 7
*Prague to Mělník*

| | |
|---|---|
| **Start** | Libeň (Prague 8), Rokytka weir (185m) |
| **Finish** | Mělník bridge (164m) |
| **Distance** | 52km |
| **Ascent** | 108m |
| **Descent** | 129m |
| **Waymarking** | Route A2 (Prague centrum–Zámcích), Route 7 (Zámcích–Mělnik) |

After leaving Prague, this stage follows the Vltava through a gorge, then climbs briefly away from the river before descending to Kralupy nad Vltavou. It then follows minor roads and field tracks to reach the confluence of the Vltava and Labe at Mělnik. There is a 100m climb at Klecany and a subsequent descent past Máslovice, otherwise the stage is flat.

### Central Prague to Libeň

If you have visited **Prague** city centre you have to retrace your route to rejoin cycleway. From NW corner of Old Town Square in centre of Prague follow nám Franze Kafty W past Sv Mikuláš church R. Turn first R (Maiselova) through Josefov (Jewish quarter). ▸ At end, turn R (Bilkova) and immediately L (Pařižská), then go-ahead past Právnická fakulta tram stop to reach riverside boulevard. Turn R (Dvořákovo nábřeži) and after 400m,

After two blocks, Maiselova becomes one-way with contra-flow cycling permitted.

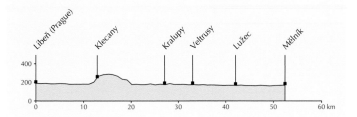

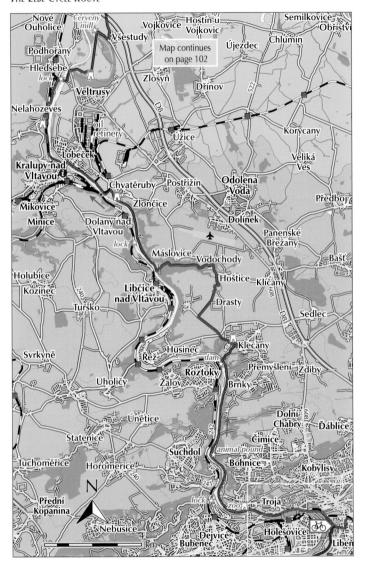

Map continues on page 102

bear L beside clocktower and descend ramp to reach riverside cycle track. Pass under three bridges, then immediately after third bridge, fork L on cinder track. Continue through post-industrial wasteland and scrubland. Just before fourth bridge, fork R to pass under bridge and go ahead on cycle track. Bear R to reach road and turn L (Menclova). After 150m, turn R on cycle track over two small bridges to reach main cycle route in **Libeň** Prague 8 (5km, 185m) (accommodation, cycle shop).

> The river **Vltava** (known as the Moldau in German) is the greatest tributary of the Elbe in both length and volume of water. Indeed, it is longer than the Elbe above their confluence at Mělnik, with their combined length of 1234km being 140km longer than the Elbe alone. The Czechs regard it as their national river and it has given its name to one of six symphonic poems composed by Bedřich Smetana that make up his masterpiece *Má Vlast* (my homeland).

**Main route continues**
Turn L through flood barrier pillars and follow cycle track between Vltava L and road R passing under railway bridge to reach motorway junction. Fork L, dropping down below bridge, then continue beside motorway R. At three-way junction before next bridge, fork L downhill to riverbank. Follow riverside track past canoe slalom course in old canal L. Bear L at road, continuing beside river past **Troja** palace R (4.5km, 182m) (accommodation, refreshments, camping).

> The Baroque palace at **Troja** was built in 1691 for the Count of Sternberg. Its central axis lines up with St Vitus cathedral which can be seen on a hilltop 3km SW. Inside, the walls and ceilings of the main rooms are highly decorated. A monumental staircase connects the palace with its French-style gardens. Since 1922, the palace has been a gallery holding Czech 19th-century paintings from the national collection.

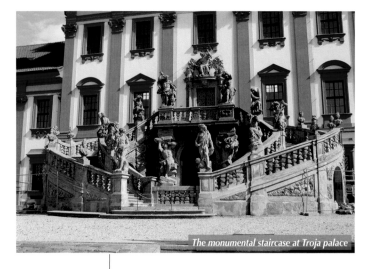

The monumental staircase at Troja palace

Ochre-coloured building R is a pound for Prague's abandoned animals.

Continue past Prague zoo R and ferry ramp at Podhoří (6km, 181m) and into gorge with hills rising beside the river, to reach Zámky (8km, 184m) (refreshments). ◀ Fork L opposite animal pound, continuing beside Vltava past Zámcích hamlet where you leave Prague and way-marks change to Route 7. Pass Klecánky ferry ramp and Klecánky hydroelectric dam, then turn R (Do Klecánek) ascending steeply and bearing R into **Klecany** (12.5km, 247m) (refreshments, cycle shop).

Turn L (nám Třebízského, then bear R (Do Kaštan), continuing uphill. Fork L (V Nových Domkách) and after 80m turn R (Spojovací) to reach T-junction. Turn L on main road (Československé Armády) across plateau. Turn R (sp Vodochody) on road through fields and winding through **Drasty** (16.5km, 277m), then descend to reach **Vodochody** (17.5km, 234m).

Turn L at beginning of village (sp Máslovice Dol), then descend steeply through woods to reach Vltava at Dol ferry (20km, 176m) (refreshments). Turn R and follow riverside gravel track past Dolany lock (21.5km, 176m) and **Chvatěruby** (23.5km, 171m) (refreshments, station).

Just before railway overbridge, turn L past sports ground then bear R beside river. Pass under railway bridge then continue past industrial area R and under pipe bridge. Emerge on road (Nábřeží J Rysa) in **Lobeček** (cycle shop) and continue ahead past village. Where road bears R, fork L dropping down to pass under road bridge. Turn L onto cycle bridge over Vltava to reach **Kralupy nad Vltavou** (27km, 174m) (accommodation, refreshments, tourist office, cycle shop, station).

The oil refinery in the industrial town of **Kralupy nad Vltavou** (pop 18,000) was attacked by allied bombers in March 1945, shortly before the end of the Second World War. Much of the town was destroyed, becoming the most heavily damaged Czech town of the war. Post-war rebuilding on Communist lines concentrated on state-owned housing, industry and a new station. For 60 years there was no central square and no town hall, though these have now been constructed.

Immediately after bridge, turn sharply R and R again, then bear L to join unsurfaced riverside track and fol-low this to **Nelahozeves** (29.5km, 174m) (accommoda-tion, refreshments, station). Turn L under railway, then R onto main road. Cycle through woods, then dog-leg R and L back over railway, following road into **Hled'sebe** (31km, 169m). Opposite factory, turn R through barri-ers on bridge/causeway across Miřejovice dam and lock. On opposite bank (accommodation, camping) turn L (Nerudova) and pass under bridge. Pass through car park, then bear R on tree-lined drive. Just before farm build-ings, fork L to pass in front of zámek **Veltrusy** palace R (33km, 172m) (refreshments).

**Veltrusy palace** was built in Baroque style with Rococo interiors for Count Chotek in 1712. It was extended in 1750 and one of the world's first trade fairs was held here in 1754. The gardens contain a number of Classical pavilions with allegorical themes, though many of these were badly damaged by floods in 2002.

Opposite front gates of palace, turn L on tree-lined drive, then continue past Červený red mill and bear R into **Všestudy** (35km, 173m). Turn L (U Zvoničky) in village and L again (Dušnická) beside house 5. Continue out of village through fields and under motorway. ◄ Bear R past **Dušníky nad Vltavou** L (37.5km, 167m) (accommodation, refreshments) and continue through Dědibaby (39km, 166m) (refreshments) to reach T-junction. Turn L and follow road through **Bukol** (41.5km, 169m) (refreshments). After 400m, turn L (sp Přívoz/Ferry) on gravel track through fields to reach Vltava and cross river by ferry to **Lužec nad Vltavou** (42.5km, 160m) (station). ◄

Bear L away from ferry to reach road and turn sharply R, passing church L. Fork R (Vltavska) and, at end of village, fork R again beside house 367 on asphalt cycle track that runs parallel with but about 100m away from river R, to reach **Vrbno** (47km, 160m).

Tall poles in fields around Dušniky are frames for hop growing.

Ferry operates 0600–1000 and 1200–1900 (Mon), 0600–1900 (Tue–Fri), 0800–1900 (Sat/Sun).

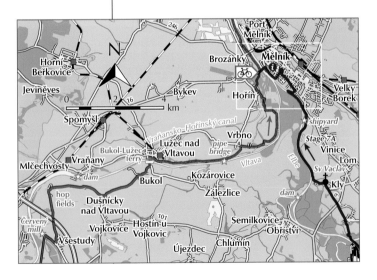

*An on-demand ferry takes cyclists across the Vltava from Bukol to Lužec*

Turn R at beginning of village, then fork R at end of village on cycle track along flood dyke to reach Vraňansko–Hořínský canal. Bear R beside canal then turn L over lock and bear R following concrete flood protection wall R into **Hořín** (51km, 163m) (refreshments).

Turn R by shrine in middle of road and R again in front of chateau. Go ahead on cycle track over small bridge and follow this winding through woods to reach stage end under **Mělník** bridge (52km, 164m). ▸

To visit Mělník (accommodation, refreshments, camping, tourist office, cycle shop, station), turn L and L again over bridge, then turn R steeply uphill to town centre.

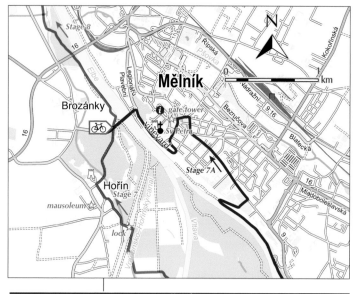

## MĚLNÍK

The old centre of Mělník (pop 19,000) sits on a bluff above the confluence of the rivers Vltava and Labe. The castle was the principal residence of dowager Bohemian queens from the early 10th until mid 15th centuries. Originally in Gothic style, it was remodelled as a Renaissance chateau in 1542 then had a Baroque wing added in 1646. For nearly 400 years, apart from 50 years in state hands during the Nazi and Communist periods, it has been owned and inhabited by the Czerin/Lobkowicz family. The church of Sv Petra a Pavla stands beside the castle. Other important buildings can be found on nám Miru Square, including the town hall. There are some remnants of the old city walls and one gate tower. Under the city is a network of caves and tunnels, a part of which can be visited.

Mělník is the centre of a small wine-producing district, with vineyards on the hillside between the castle and the Labe and wine cellars under the castle. It produces mostly white wines from müller thurgau, grüner veltliner and riesling grapes.

# STAGE 7A
*Lázně Toušeň to Mělník (avoiding Prague)*

| | |
|---|---|
| **Start** | Lázně Toušeň, Na Krétě (172m) |
| **Finish** | Mělník bridge (164m) |
| **Distance** | 33.5km |
| **Waymarking** | Route 2 |

This short stage enables cyclists to avoid Prague by following the Labe through the former royal town of Brandýs nad Labem directly to Mělník. It is mostly on riverside tracks and is flat except for a short steep climb into Mělník near the end.

From path junction with Stage 6 in **Lázně Toušeň**, follow riverside cycle track NW past industrial area L. Cycle under motorway bridge, then just before Stará Boreslav hydroelectric dam, fork L and walk bike up zig-zag boardwalk to reach road. Turn R into **Brandýs nad Labem** (3.5km, 174m) (accommodation, refreshments, tourist office, cycle shop, station).

The castle at **Brandýs nad Labem** (pop 12,000) became the property of the Austrian Habsburg throne in 1547. Favoured by Emperor Ferdinand II as a royal country residence, the original Gothic castle was redeveloped into a sumptuous Renaissance palace with sgraffito-etched plaster decoration. Subsequent Habsburg emperors all inhabited the castle. Rudolf II used it as a summer palace and Charles VI as a hunting lodge. In 1813, Emperor Francis I met the Kaiser and Tsar here to agree a plan to fight Napoleon, while the last Habsburg Emperor Charles I was living here with his wife Zita at the outbreak of the First World War. Their apartments have been renovated and can be visited.

*Brandýs nad Labem castle was the residence of Austro-Hungarian Emperor Charles I in 1914*

Turn R opposite castle, crossing mill stream, and turn L beside Labe. Pass under road bridge and follow cycle track ahead through woodland. Recross millstream then dog-leg away from Labe around recreation area. Return to riverside track and continue to **Záryby** (9km, 167m) (refreshments).

Turn R at T-junction. After 1.5km, bear L away from river on winding track through fields. Emerge on road and turn R over small bridge. Turn L at T-junction (Na Pískách), then sharply R (K Elektráně) at road junction in **Kostelec nad Labem** (12km, 169m) (cycle shop, station).

After 200m, turn L on cycle track through fields and woods. Emerge on main road and turn R, following road bridge over Labe. ◀ On opposite bank, turn L on rough track beside river. Pass weekend home estate in woodland R, then turn L to continue beside Labe, passing **Kozly** R (17km, 164m). Continue on riverside track to reach road just before Lobkovice lock and bear R (Hlavní) away from river into Mlékojedy (19km, 164m).

*This is a busy main road with no cycle lane.*

Turn L on narrow road (K Jezu) beside house 5 returning to riverbank. Cycle under railway bridge then continue past Neratovice and huge Spolana chemical works on opposite bank. Track winds through scrubland then passes under two conveyer bridges and pipe bridge. ▶ After end of chemical works, follow track bearing R away from Labe into woods then turn R along flood dyke through fields. Pass sports club R, then bear R at crossing of tracks and R for **Tuhaň** (24km, 165m).

This is a spoil deposit area for the chemical works.

Turn R at T-junction, then after 40m turn L at crossroads and continue out of village to soon reach **Větrušice** (24.5km, 162m). Go ahead over main road following track through fields to T-junction., then bear L to reach Sv Vaclav chapel in middle of road in **Kly** (25.5km, 163m) (refreshments).

Turn L through village back to riverbank and continue on riverside asphalt track for 2km. Bear R away from Labe

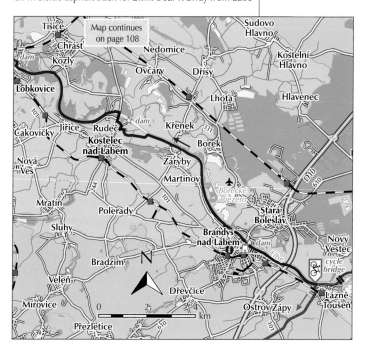

Map continues on page 108

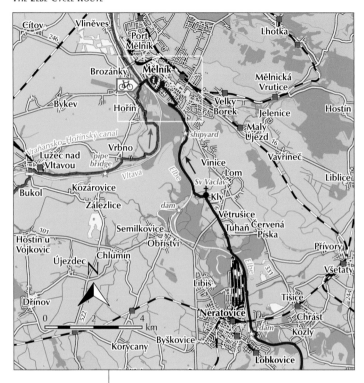

For description and urban map of Mělník see Stage 7.

on gravel track through woods. Pass small shipyard L then continue close to river with beginning of Mělník on ridgetop above R. Turn sharply R, uphill away from river. Bear R and turn L across ridgetop track then pass football pitch L to reach main road. Turn L (Pražská) into **Mělník** (32km, 214m) (accommodation, refreshments, camping, tourist office, cycle shop, station). ◄

Where road ahead becomes one-way, fork R (Fibichova) to reach T-junction. Turn L and continue into náměstí Karla IV Square, then turn L to leave square by opposite corner (Jaroslava Seiferta). Follow this, bearing L then turn R at T-junction (K Mostu). Bear R descending through hillside vineyards with confluence of rivers

*Sv Vaclav roadside chapel in Kly*

Vltava and Labe below L and castle on hilltop above R. Turn L and cross bridge over Labe. After crossing river, but still on bridge, turn sharply R, dropping down to join route via Prague (at beginning of Stage 8) (33.5km, 164m).

# STAGE 8
### Mělník to Litoměřice

| | |
|---|---|
| **Start** | Mělník bridge (164m) |
| **Finish** | Litoměřice bridge (152m) |
| **Distance** | 47km |
| **Waymarking** | Route 2 (Mělník–Roudnice), 2a (Roudnice–Litoměřice) |

A flat stage that closely follows the left bank of the Labe, either on riverside cycle tracks or nearby quiet roads. Towards the end, a detour is made to pass through the walled fortress town of Terezín that gained infamy during the Second World War as the site of Theresienstadt Nazi concentration camp.

From track junction beside **Mělník** bridge, follow riverside cycle track N beside Labe. Cycle under road bridge then follow track through woods away from river. Cross side-stream, then continue beside river past Port Mělnik

Labe flood marker at Dolní Beřkovice shows 2002 flood over 9m above normal level

harbour across river R and **Vliněves** L (3km, 161m) (refreshments). ▸ Cycle under pipe bridge and past **Dolní Beřkovice** (5km, 161m) (refreshments, station).

Opposite entrance to Liběchov lock, turn sharply L away from river then R to pass lock cottages R. At end of lock, bear L parallel with river and pass huge Mělník coal-fired power station. Cross two cooling water outlet streams, then bear L away from Labe and R through fields. Follow track back to river and pass **Horni Počaply**

Port Mělnik is the principal commercial harbour of Czechia.

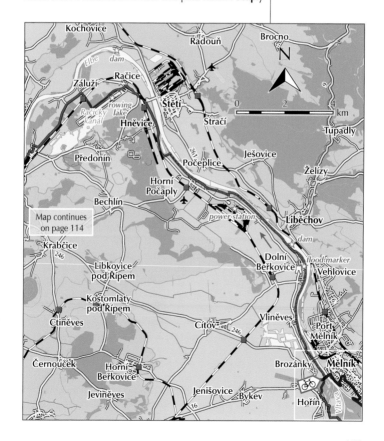

(11.5km, 155m) (accommodation, refreshments, station). After 1km, turn L away from Labe then R onto quiet road and follow this through **Hnévice** (14.5km, 156m) (station). Follow road bearing L under railway bridge, then turn R on road into **Račice** (16.5km, 160m) (accommodation, refreshments).

> Old aggregates pits at **Račice** (pop 350) have been used to create an eight-lane by 2000m international standard rowing lake that held the world championships in 1986 and 1993. It has also hosted European and junior rowing championships and the canoeing world championship. Nearby lakes are used for fishing and have held the world fishing competition.

At crossroads in village turn L beside house 26 (sp Labe aréna Račice), then continue past competitors' centre and grandstands of rowing lake L. Where road ends, go ahead on gravel track beside lake, then turn R away from lake through woods and across railway into **Záluží** (19.5km, 159m) (station). Turn L at crossroads and follow road to beginning of built-up area. Turn R (Krajní), then L at T-junction (K Přívozu) to reach middle of **Dobříň** (23km, 153m) (accommodation, station).

Turn R (Horova) by yellow bus shelter with clock on top. Fork second R, past bandstand R, and bear immediately L, then turn L following road behind houses and out of village. Continue on cycle track beside Labe passing station R and under road bridge in **Roudnice nad Labem** (25.5km, 152m) (accommodation, refreshments, tourist office, cycle shop, station).

> **Roudnice nad Labem** (pop 13,000) grew up beside the oldest bridge over the Labe in Bohemia. The original stone bridge was destroyed (1634) by Swedish troops during the Thirty Years' War and not reinstated until 1910 when an art nouveau iron bridge was built. The first castle overlooking the bridge was built in Romanesque style during the

12th century. Damaged during the Hussite Wars, the remains were incorporated into a Renaissance palace in the late 16th century. This lasted about 100 years before suffering damage in the Thirty Years' War and being replaced (1684) by a Baroque chateau which became the primary residence of the Lobkowicz family. Parts of all three buildings are incorporated in the present-day structure. During the Communist period it housed a military academy, before being returned to Lobkowicz ownership in 1989.

*Roudnice castle is the ancestral home of the Lobkowicz family*

Pass behind buildings at Roudnice lock, then continue beside river past **Židovice** (28.5km, 156m). At **Hrobce** (31km, 154m) (refreshments, station), bear L away from river and follow road (K Labi) curving L into village centre. Go ahead over crossroads (Hlavní), then turn R (Lipová). Where road ends, continue ahead on cycle track through fields and woods to reach T-junction in **Libotenice** (33km, 155m) (refreshments).

Turn R, then L beside house 88. Go ahead R over five-way crossroads. Turn L at T-junction and follow road

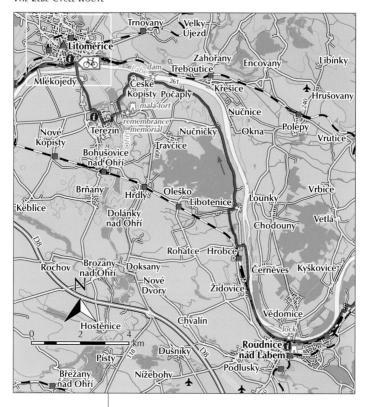

out of village through fields planted with hops, to reach **Nučničky** (36km, 152m). Fork R beside house 9, then continue through fields to **Počaply** (38.5km, 151m). Go ahead at crossroads in village, continuing on quiet road through fields. At beginning of **České Kopisty** (41.5km, 147m) fork R to reach river beside lock.

Follow road, curving L through village, then turn R before house 106. Continue through fields and trees to T-junction beside car and bus park for Terezín. ◄ Turn R, crossing river Ohře, then L in front of main bastion fortifications. Turn R (cobbles) over former moat

*Turn L past memorial gardens and cemetery to reach Terezín small fort.*

and pass through arch. Bear R and turn immediately L (Palackého), then turn third R (Prokopa Holého) to reach nám Československé Armády Square in centre of **Terezín** (43.5km, 152m) (accommodation, refreshments, camping, tourist office, cycle shop).

## TEREZÍN

Terezín (pop 2900), known as Theresienstadt in German, was a twin fortress to Josefov (passed on Stage 3). Named after the Empress Maria Theresa, it was built (1780–1790) to protect the Austrian empire from Prussian invasion, but never fired a shot in anger. It took 15,000 men laying 20 million bricks, 10 years to build a fort with barracks for 11,000 soldiers. The defensive system consisted of two forts on either side of the river Ohře, the rectangular *mala* (small) fort on the east bank and the octagonal *hlavní* (main) fort on the west, with the river being diverted during construction to provide a moat for the main fort. Inside the walls, the 11 barracks, armouries and civilian buildings were built with thick walls to withstand artillery bombardment. The military presence ended in 1990, since when parts of the complex have found civilian use. Some conservation work has been done, but preserving a site this size is a nearly impossible task, particularly since the site was badly damaged by flooding in 2002.

During the Second World War, the small fort served as a gestapo (German Nazi secret police) prison mostly for political prisoners. The main fort was used by the Nazis as an enclosed ghetto for Jewish people who were brought here from Prague and other parts of the country for incarceration until being sent to their deaths at extermination camps like Auschwitz in Poland. In total 88,135 people went from Theresienstadt to die in death camps. Since the war, a memorial has been established to commemorate victims of the atrocities.

Continue past square into Máchova to reach T-junction. Turn L (Akademická), then at next T-junction turn R through main fortifications and follow road bearing L. Turn R beside end of Terezín sign and continue past golf course to reach main road. Bear R and cycle over Labe to reach T-junction beside river in **Litoměřice** (47km, 152m) (accommodation, youth hostel, refreshments, camping, tourist office, cycle shop, station).

Prior to 1945, **Litoměřice** (pop 24,000) was a majority German-speaking town in the Sudetenland along the border between Bohemia and Germany. It grew to medieval prosperity as the main Bohemian port on the Labe where German traders had to stop and offer their products for sale before entering Austrian imperial lands. Mirové nám Square is surrounded by historic buildings, including some of the oldest inhabited buildings in Czechia. The town hall is in Saxon Renaissance style, while another Renaissance building, the dům U Černého Orla (Black Eagle house), is extensively decorated with sgrafitti. The town lost out with the arrival of industry in the 19th century. A paucity of flood-free flat land, led to industry developing downriver at Ústí nad Labem, which replaced Litoměřice as the main commercial town of the region. The Sudeten German population was expelled in 1945 and replaced with Czech-speaking peoples.

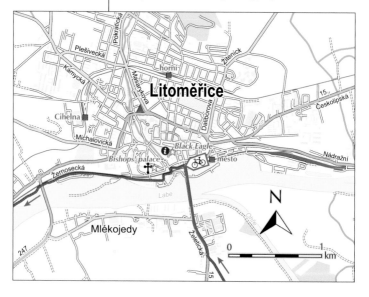

# STAGE 9
*Litoměřice to Děčín*

| | |
|---|---|
| **Start** | Litoměřice bridge (152m) |
| **Finish** | Děčín bridge (130m) |
| **Distance** | 50.5km |
| **Waymarking** | Route 2 |

A generally level stage that follows the right bank of the Labe through the Porta Bohemica gorge past the industrial city of Ústí nad Labem on the opposite bank. Most of the route is on dedicated cycle tracks, either by the river or beside nearby roads and railways.

From T-junction at N end of **Litoměřice** bridge, follow cobbled Stará Mostecká W downhill. Continue into **Vodní**, passing below city walls. At end, turn L (Jarošova) under railway then immediately R (Labská) beside railway. Follow road round zig-zags L and R then continue through allotments. Pass swimming pool complex and sewage plant (both L). Where road ends, continue ahead on cycle track under bridge, with Labe L and railway R to reach **Žalhostice** (3.5km, 148km) (refreshments, station).

Go ahead over crossroads (do not cross railway) and continue to T-junction. Turn L then follow road zig-zagging R and L under railway into beginning of **Píšťany** hamlet (accommodation, refreshments). Turn R beside house 56 to reach road, then fork R uphill, passing concrete works L. Where road turns R over railway, continue ahead on cycle track between concrete works L and railway R. Pass **Velké Žernoseky** (7km, 145m) (accommodation, refreshments, station) and continue between Labe L and railway R past station to **Libochovany** (11km, 151m) (refreshments, station). Follow road winding through village and at end of village continue beside railway R.

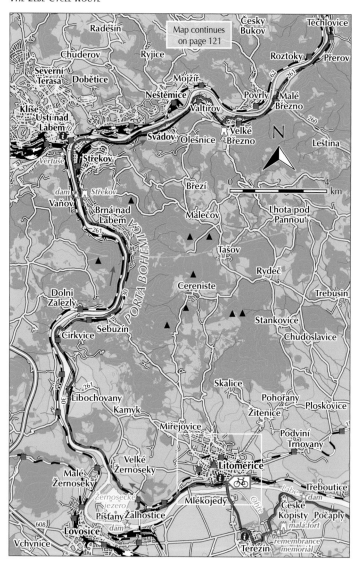

Map continues
on page 121

Emerge onto road at loading point for roadstone quarry and continue ahead on cycle track L of road. Fork L on cycle track, descending to riverbank and follow this into **Cirkvice** (14km, 147m).

Turn first R before house 13, then fork L to reach main road. Dog-leg L and R across road, then continue uphill over railway bridge and turn L parallel with railway. Continue to crossing of tracks and turn L under railway, then turn R at T-junction into **Sebuzín** (16.5km, 152m) (refreshments, cycle shop, station).

Dog-leg R and L over crossroads past small chapel R, then descend through village. Just before reaching main road, bear R on service road and, where this ends, continue on cycle track bearing R away from main road. After 100m, turn L and cross main road to reach cycle track between Labe L and road R. Emerge beside main road and continue on cycle track beside road R. Fork L away from road then turn L at T-junction and continue beside river past **Brná nad Labem** (19.5k, 144m) (accommodation, refreshments, camping).

Pass swimming pool complex L, then turn R uphill under bridge and immediately sharply L beside railway. Emerge on road and fork L to continue following railway to reach T-junction. ▶ Bear L onto main road and pass **Střekov** lock and dam L (22.5km, 145m) (refreshments, station) with Střekov castle on clifftop R.

> Ignore Route 2 signs taking you L under railway as this involves three flights of stairs over Střekov dam.

**Střekov castle**'s position perched on a cliff overlooking a bend of the river is one of the most dramatic on the whole Labe/Elbe system. It was built in 1316 for John of Luxembourg (father of Emperor Charles IV) to guard the Germany–Bohemia riverside trade route. The Lobkowicz family acquired the castle in 1563 and, despite occupations by Habsburgs, Saxons, Swedes, Prussians, German Nazis and Communists, it is now back in family hands. Badly damaged during the Thirty Years' and Seven Years' Wars, it was abandoned as a military structure. During the 19th century, the ruins attracted writers and artists including Goethe, who

*Střekov castle was built for John of Luxembourg in 1316*

To visit Ústí nad Labem (accommodation, refreshments, tourist office, cycle shop, station) on opposite bank, take R fork and turn L over second bridge.

described the view as the most beautiful in central Europe, and Wagner, who used it as an inspiration for his opera *Tannhäuser*.

After 350m, turn L under railway and turn R to continue beside river. Where track divides, fork L on lower track closer to river. ◄ Continue under rail and two road bridges, then follow red brick block cycle track under third bridge and curve R beside slip road. Bear L to continue beside main road and where cycle track ends, cross road to reach cycle lane R. After 1.5km, recross road and fork L past **Svádov** (29km, 134m) (accommodation, station) then fork L again at end of village to reach road and continue on cycle track to **Valtířov** (31km, 142m) (refreshments, station).

Ascend steeply and turn L at top. Fork R opposite cemetery through village and into open country. Just before railway crossing, fork L on cycle track beside railway to reach road in **Velké Březno** (33km, 136m) (refreshments, station). Turn L, then fork R and after 100m fork L

120

and follow cycle track circling edge of village. Emerge on road and turn L to reach Labe, then follow riverside cycle track to **Malé Březno** (35.5km, 135m) (station).

Cross Luční potok stream then, just before railway crossing, turn sharply L to continue on cycle track beside railway. Follow this back to Labe at **Přerov** (38km 131m) then continue past **Těchlovice** (39km, 132m) (station) and **Boletice nad Labem** (44.5km, 130m) (station). Follow track bearing R away from river, then turn L beside railway. At **Křešice**, follow track winding through scrubland to reach Labe and continue below beginning of Děčín. Fork L to continue beside river, then bear L at T-junction. Just before major road bridge, fork R away from river and cross medieval bridge over river Ploučnice. Immediately after bridge, turn sharply L beneath slip roads from road bridge and follow Ploučnice L to its confluence with Labe. Continue under railway bridge and pass castle high

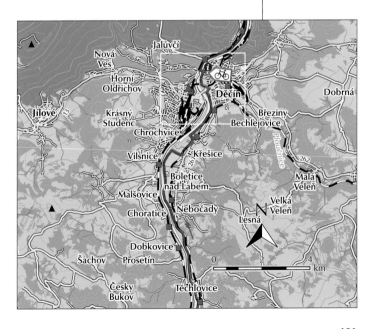

121

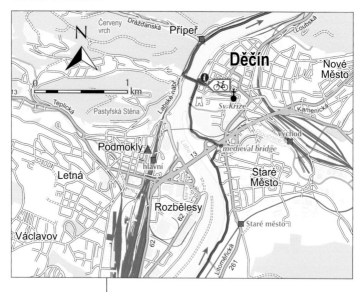

*Děčín castle has a commanding position above the Labe*

above R. Go under road bridge, then turn R beside bridge to reach end of stage in **Děčín** (50.5km, 130m) (accommodation, youth hostel, refreshments, camping, tourist office, cycle shop, station).

## DĚČÍN

*Medieval Ploučnice bridge in Děčín*

Děčín (pop 49,000) spreads across both banks of the Labe, with the old city on the right bank and the industrial district of Podmokly on the left. The Baroque castle on a bluff beside the bridge is the dominant feature. Originally built as a wooden castle (about AD993) it metamorphized over the centuries through Gothic stone castle and Renaissance palace to the Baroque structure seen today, which was completed in 1803. Its most notable features are a slender clock tower on the riverfront and a long drive cut through sandstone that gives access from the town centre. The castle was owned by the Thun family from 1628 to 1932, when financial problems caused them to sell it to the Czechoslovak state. Converted to a military barracks, it housed Czech, German then Russian troops until 1991. Restoration commenced in 2000 and much of the castle is now open to visitors. Other significant buildings include the Baroque church of Sv Krize beside the castle drive, a medieval stone bridge over the Ploučnice and a restored synagogue.

# STAGE 10
*Děčín to Bad Schandau*

| | |
|---|---|
| **Start** | Děčín bridge (130m) |
| **Finish** | Bad Schandau, ferry ramp (120m) |
| **Distance** | 21km |
| **Waymarking** | Czech Route 2 (Děčín–border); Deutsches Radweg D10 (border to Bad Schandau) |

This short stage has the most spectacular scenery of the whole journey. The route crosses to the left bank and follows a riverside cycle track through a narrow gorge lined by towering weathered sandstone crags. About halfway through the gorge, the German border is reached and the route continues beside the river (now called the Elbe) before using a ferry to reach the spa town of Bad Schandau.

From road junction by approach to Tyršův most bridge in **Děčín**, cycle W over bridge across Labe. Turn R on riverside road, then fork R beside **Přípeř** station (station), continuing along riverside. Pass under railway bridge at Horní Žleb (2.5km, 129m), then continue on cycle track through woods with railway L and Labe R past Prostřední Žleb and Čertova Voda (5.5km, 124m) (station). Continue past ferry ramp at Dolní Žleb (8.5km, 125m) (refreshments, station) then enter Germany at **Czech/German border** (10.5km, 124m). ◄

*For next 3.5km, the border runs mid-stream down the river with Czechia still on left bank.*

Pass Schöna–Hřensko ferry ramp (12.5km, 124m) (station) then Hirschmühle–Schmilka ferry ramp (14.5km, 124m) (station) at point where German territory begins on opposite bank. Continue to **Krippen** (19.5km, 121m) (accommodation, refreshments, station), then cross Elbe using Krippen–Postelwitz ferry to Postelwitz (accommodation, cycle shop) on opposite bank. ◄

*Ferry operates weekdays 0613–2243, weekends 0813–2243 with frequent services between 13 and 43 minutes past every hour.*

Follow riverside cycle track over river Kirnitzsch and past Ostrau lift then thermal spa complex (both L)

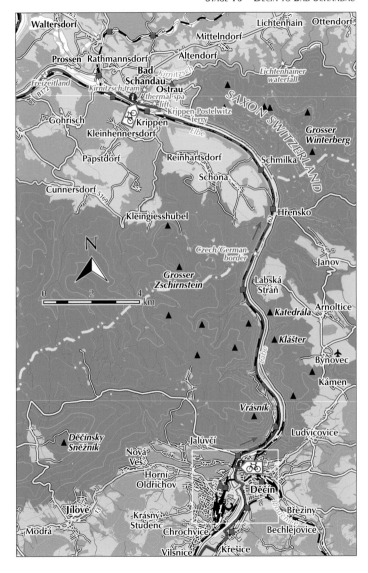

*A ferry takes you across the river from Krippen to Postelwitz to visit Bad Schandau*

to reach road head by ferry ramp and car park in centre of **Bad Schandau** (21km, 120m) (accommodation, youth hostel, refreshments, tourist office, cycle shop, station).

**Bad Schandau** (pop 3600) is a spa town squeezed into the Elbe gorge beneath sandstone cliffs and running up the narrow Kirnitzsch valley. Originally founded as a riverside trading post before 1437, the town became popular as a spa resort after 1799. The riverfront is dominated by the Elbresidenz hotel (previously the Dampfschiff which was completely rebuilt after being badly damaged by floods in 2002) and nearby Johanniskirche (St John's church) with a Renaissance two-storey sandstone altar. Behind the hotel, Marktplatz has Renaissance buildings and an art nouveau fountain. Ostrau, on the hilltop overlooking the town, is connected by a 50m outdoor lift in art nouveau style. A tramway runs from the town 8km up the Kirnitzsch valley to waterfalls at Lichtenhaimer.

*A lift, in art nouveau style, takes visitors up to Ostrau village above Bad Schandau*

# STAGE 11
*Bad Schandau to Dresden*

| | |
|---|---|
| **Start** | Bad Schandau, ferry ramp (120m) |
| **Finish** | Dresden, Augustusbrücke (108m) |
| **Distance** | 46km |
| **Waymarking** | D10 and Elberadweg |

A mostly flat stage of two parts. First the route continues through the gorge of 'Saxon Switzerland' with the Bastei rocks high above the river, then it enters the suburbs of Dresden and follows riverside paths into the city centre.

**Saxon Switzerland** is an area of sandstone mountains that straddle the border between Czechia and the Saxon region of Germany. The name was first coined in the late 18th century by two Swiss artists working at Dresden Academy of Art who wrote comparing the Elbe sandstone mountains with their homeland in the Swiss Jura. Their description was subsequently used by writer Wilhelm Götzinger in his books about the area and the name has stuck.

Along the Elbe valley, sheer sandstone cliffs rise up beside the river and in many places these have become weathered into fantastic shapes. The most famous of these are the Bastei rocks, above the right bank of the Elbe opposite Oberrathen, where a series of rock pinnacles are connected by a sandstone bridge.

From ferry ramp in **Bad Schandau**, follow riverside road (An der Elbe) NW past car park and bus station. Where road ends, continue ahead on cycle track then fork R beside Lidl supermarket R. Turn L on main road (Basteistrasse) then follow this forking L on bridge over Elbe. Immediately after bridge, turn L at crossroads

The Bastei rock bridge is the most stunning view in Saxon Switzerland

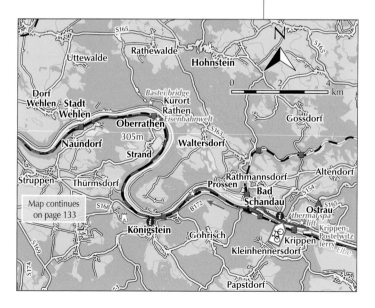

Map continues
on page 133

then take third exit at roundabout (sp Reinhardtsdorf). Opposite station, turn sharply L on riverside cycle track and continue under road and railway bridges. Follow track bearing L away from river, then turn R beside railway passing Elbe Freizeitland amusement park R (5.5km, 124m) (camping). Continue past campsite R and **Königstein** station L (7.5km, 119m) (accommodation, refreshments, camping, tourist office, cycle shop, station). ◄

*To visit Königstein, turn L under station bridge.*

The fortress of **Königstein** (pop 2000) is one of the largest hilltop fortifications in Europe. First started in 1589 and added to frequently until 1895, it occupies a 10-hectare plateau, 240m above the Elbe. The outer walls are up to 42m high and extend for 1.8km around the plateau. There are over 50 buildings within the fortress representing over 400 years of civilian and military activity. The well at the centre goes down 152.5m, the second deepest in Europe. As a fortress, it was never captured; however, in 1756 the Saxon ruler Frederick Augustus II could only watch from the battlements as his army was surrounded by the Prussians and surrendered on the riverbank opposite the fortress. When it lost its military role, the fortress became a prison used to hold 'enemies of the state' and prisoners of war in both world wars. It also served as a repository for state reserves, archives and art treasures during periods of war. Nowadays it is a tourist attraction visited by 700,000 people annually.

Continue on cycle track between railway L and Elbe R, passing below festung Königstein castle on hilltop L. Dog-leg L and R under railway at **Thürmsdorf** (accommodation, refreshments) then continue beside railway R through **Strand** (11km, 122m). After 1.2km, follow road R across railway and L through fields to reach road junction. Go ahead past Eisenbahnwelten L and bear L across railway in **Oberrathen** (13.5km, 121m) (accommodation, refreshments, station). ◄

*Eisenbahnwelt (railway world) is an enormous outdoor model railway system.*

Bear R at road junction and continue through woods to **Pötzscha** (16.5km, 125m) (accommodation, refreshments, station). Emerge onto road and pass railway station R, then continue on cycle track between wooded hillside L and railway R. Dog-leg R and L under railway and follow riverside track to Obervogelgesang (20km, 114m) (refreshments, station). Continue between railway L and Elbe R, ignoring all turns L under railway, to reach roundabout before boat landing stage in **Pirna** (24km, 113m) (accommodation, youth hostel – in Copitz on R bank – refreshments, camping, tourist office, cycle shop, station). ▶

*Pirna town hall is a mix of gothic, renaissance and Baroque styles*

*To visit centre of Pirna, turn L under railway.*

The old centre of **Pirna** (pop 38,000) consists of a grid pattern of streets grouped around Am Markt Square with an attractive town hall and St Marien church. The town is overlooked by Sonnenstein fortress on Burgberg hill. An 11th-century castle was upgraded to a fortress in 1544. After capture and devastation by Swedish troops in the Thirty Years' War, it was rebuilt (1670) as a modern military fortress and parts of these fortifications still stand. In 1811 it lost its military role and became a mental hospital. Under the Nazis this was used (1940-42) as a euthanasia killing centre where about 15,000 disabled people were gassed. This was the first use of techniques later used to kill six million people

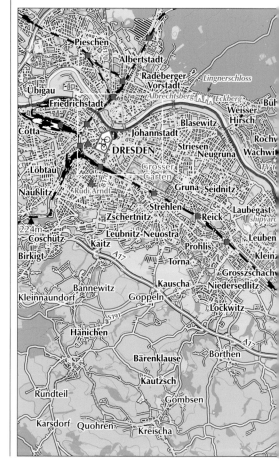

in concentration camp gas chambers. A plaque and memorial stand in remembrance of these atrocities.

Pass boat landing stages R, then fork R on cycle track passing under road bridge and motorway bridge. Continue beside main road, then fork R past **Heidenau**

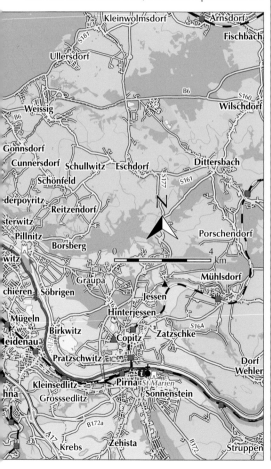

133

(28km, 116m) (accommodation, refreshments, cycle shop, station). Cross river Müglitz and pass Heidenau–Birkwitz ferry ramp. Eventually bear L away from river to reach T-junction in **Zschieren** (31.5km, 112m) (accommodation, refreshments). Turn R and continue past Pillnitz palace on opposite bank then go ahead over ferry ramp in **Kleinzschachwitz** (33.5km, 115m) (accommodation, refreshments, camping). Emerge beside main road and bear R on dual use footpath/cycle track (Österreicher Strasse) passing shipyard R. ◄ After shipyard, turn R by bus stop and return to riverbank (R turn is easily missed), then follow riverside cycle track past **Laubegast** (35.5km, 117m) (accommodation, refreshments).

Laubegast shipyard builds and maintains the fleet of Elbe pleasure boats.

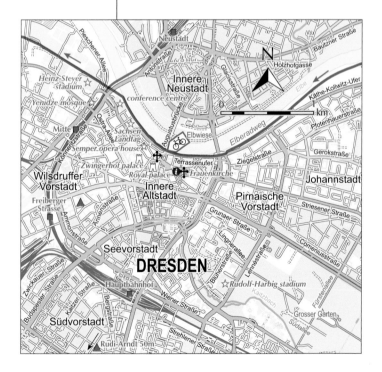

Pass Dresden TV mast towering over opposite bank and cycle through riverside meadows past Dresden suburbs of **Neugruna** and **Blasewitz** (40km, 111m) (accommodation, refreshments). Fork R to pass under Loschwitzbrücke bridge and continue past grassy flood plain. Pass under two more bridges, then bear R beside main road and pass under next bridge to reach end of stage after 600m by Augustusbrücke bridge in centre of **Dresden** (46km, 108m) (accommodation, youth hostel, refreshments, tourist office, cycle shop, station). ▶

To reach Schlossplatz, fork L before bridge on cobbled ramp up to bridge.

## DRESDEN

*The neo-Renaissance Semper opera house in Dresden was built in 1878*

To many people, Dresden (pop 550,000) is best known for the events of 13 February 1945 when the inner city was largely destroyed by over 2500 tons of bombs dropped by 773 RAF Lancaster bombers. The ensuing firestorm resulted in 18,000–25,000 fatalities. However, the city has a history going back 800 years as the capital of Saxony and residence of the Elector (ruler). A large number of Baroque and Rococo buildings led to the city centre being known as the 'jewel box'. Most of these were built during the reigns of Augustus II (1694–1733) and Augustus III (1734–1763), including the

*Dresden's Frauenkirche re-opened in 2005 after restoration from destruction in the 1945 bombing*

Zwingerhof royal palace and two prominent churches, the wedding-cake tiered Hofkirche (Catholic cathedral) and domed Frauenkirche (Lutheran). Most of these buildings were destroyed in the bombing. During the post-war period rebuilding and restoration was patchy. Some buildings were restored, others (including the Frauenkirche) were left in ruins as grim war memorials while some were swept away and replaced by socialist 'modern-style' concrete buildings. Since reunification, restoration has begun anew and, although there are still a few areas where damage is evident, almost all the inner city has been reborn. The highlight was the completion of the Frauenkirche in 2005 topped with a gold cross paid for by 'the British people and the house of Windsor'. Dresden is a very green city with large areas of parks, gardens and even forest within its boundaries. The most notable is the Grosser Garten, which includes parks, zoo, childrens' railway and a football stadium.

# STAGE 12
### Dresden to Meissen

| | |
|---|---|
| **Start** | Dresden, Augustusbrücke (108m) |
| **Finish** | Meissen, Altstadtbrücke (101m) |
| **Distance** | 25.5km |
| **Waymarking** | Elberadweg |

After leaving Dresden's suburbs, this almost completely level stage follows the left bank of the Elbe, mostly on cycle tracks through fields or beside flood dykes, passing a series of small villages to reach the porcelain manufacturing town of Meissen.

From beneath Augustusbrücke bridge in **Dresden**, follow riverside cycle path NW past modern Sachsen Landtag (regional parliament building), Maritim hotel and

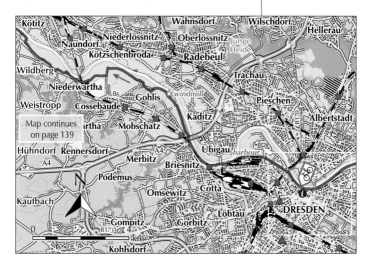

*The Yenidze mosque in Dresden was converted from a former tobacco factory*

If you look L before the stadium you will see a large mosque that has been converted from an old tobacco factory.

international conference centre (all L). Follow cycle track bearing L away from river under road and rail bridges and continue on Rudolf-Harbig-Weg past Heinz-Steyer stadium and indoor sports arena (both L). ◀ Cycle under another bridge then continue past Dresden harbour L and cross bridge over harbour mouth. Follow track beside road L, then bear R across side road and continue under road bridge. Cross bridge over side river and continue between railway L and Elbe R, passing under motorway bridge. Go ahead on cycle track through riverside meadows, then dog-leg L and R at crossing of tracks. Pass preserved windmill R, then continue winding through fields and pass through gap in flood dyke to reach road head in **Gohlis** (9km, 107m) (accommodation, refreshments).

Continue to crossroads and turn R (Elbstrasse) to reach T-junction. Turn R (Dorfstrasse) and follow this to end of village, then go ahead through another flood dyke gap and continue beside river R. Follow cycle track bearing L beside decorated pumping station, then

turn R and pass electricity sub-station L. Turn R at crossing of tracks and pass under railway and road bridges at
**Niederwartha** (12.5km, 106m) (refreshments, station).
Cross small stream and turn R at T-junction and follow
cycle track passing village L. After cycling beside road for
short distance, bear R to pass behind houses of **Wildberg**
(14.5km, 108m) (accommodation, refreshments).

At end of village, bear R and continue through fields.
Just before first buildings of **Constappel** (16km, 106m)
(accommodation, refreshments), turn R then dog-leg L
and R over small stream. Bear L beside Elbe and go ahead
over crossing of tracks by Gauernitz–Kötitz ferry, then
continue on riverside track to reach road in **Gauernitz**
(17.5km, 105m). Bear R then follow cycle track winding
through village and continue through fields to Reppina
hamlet (19.5km, 103m) (accommodation, refreshments).

Follow cycle track dog-legging L and R, then continue
parallel with road past Rehbocktal (refreshments, camping) and **Siebeneichen** castle (23.5km, 103m) (refreshments). Continue on cycle track beside main road under

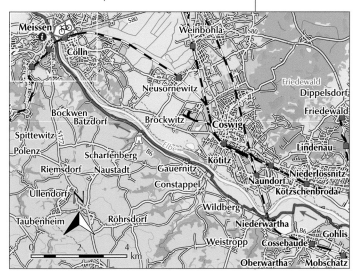

railway bridge to stage end just before Altstadtbrücke bridge in **Meissen** (25.5km, 101m) (accommodation, refreshments, tourist office, cycle shop, station).

## MEISSEN

*The Royal Meissen factory has been producing high-quality porcelain since 1710*

The name of Meissen (pop 28,000) is synonymous with fine porcelain. Extensive local deposits of china clay and potter's earth led King Augustus II to establish a porcelain factory within the Albrechtsburg royal castle in 1710, the first high-quality porcelain to be produced outside the Orient. In 1863 the factory moved to Triebischtal, 1km SW from the centre, where it still operates and can be visited.

The town, one of the oldest on the Elbe, was founded in AD929 and is regarded as the cradle of Saxony. The Gothic cathedral (built 1260–1410) is one of the smallest in Europe. Its twin spires were added in 1910. The Albrectsburg castle (built 1472–1525), which shares the same hill above the river, became the residence of Duke Albert of Saxony after 1485 and was the first in Germany to be used only as a royal residence with no military function. Below the hill, Markt Square has Renaissance buildings and the Frauenkirche with a carillon of porcelain bells commissioned in 1929 for the 1000th anniversary of the city.

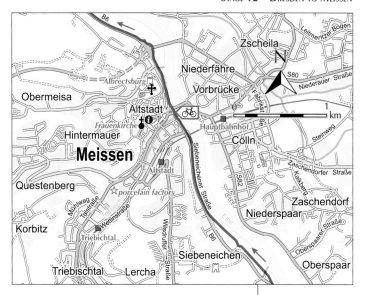

# STAGE 13
## *Meissen to Riesa*

| | |
|---|---|
| **Start** | Meissen, Altstadtbrücke (101m) |
| **Finish** | Riesa, Elbstrasse (108m) |
| **Distance** | 25.5km |
| **Waymarking** | Elberadweg |

This stage is mostly flat with a few gentle undulations. It uses asphalt cycle tracks that follow the Elbe, run beside nearby roads or follow flood dykes, something that will become increasingly common for the remainder of the journey. A few very small villages are passed but no towns.

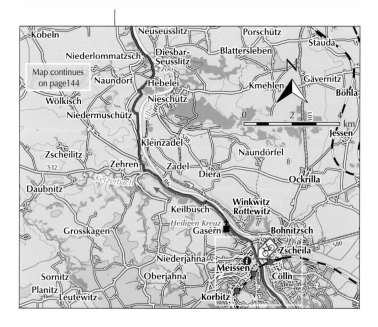

Map continues on page 144

From Altstadtbrücke bridge in **Meissen**, follow riverside cycle track N under bridge and continue through car park below main road L. Fork R (sp Festplatz) to pass under next bridge, then continue past gardens and ruins of Heiligen Kreuz monastery L. Cross small bridge, then bear L to reach **Keilbusch** (3.5km,103m) (refreshments). Turn R on cycle track beside main road, then after 1.5km fork R beside bus stop and continue ahead on cycle track. Turn R across small bridge over Ketzerbach stream then R again at path junction. Turn L through gates, passing sports hall R to reach main road in centre of **Zehren** (7km, 102m) (accommodation).

Turn R, then where main road bears L, fork R on quiet road (Niedermuschützer Strasse) past fire station R. At end of village fork R on cycle track leading to Zehren–Kleinzadel ferry. Before ferry ramp, fork L on riverside cycle track and follow this bearing L away from Elbe past **Niedermuschütz** (9.5km, 100m). At Stauden Ihm, pass under lattice bridge and ascend narrow coombe through plant nursery. Turn R at T-junction and continue over slight ridge, then descend to reach road. Fork L through **Hebelei** (accommodation) and pass small

*The Elbe cycle route near Zehren*

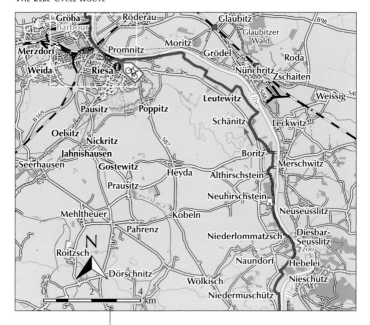

The Radhaus guest house in Niederlommatzsch caters mainly for cyclists.

Belgian King Leopold III was interned in Neuhirschstein castle during the Second World War.

*tiergarten* (zoo) R, then continue to reach ferry ramp in **Niederlommatzsch** (12km, 98m) (accommodation, refreshments). ◄

Turn L away from river, then immediately R (Hirschsteiner Weg) opposite Elbklause hotel. Follow cobbled road beside Elbe to reach **Neuhirschstein** (13.5km, 98m) (refreshments) and fork R, passing castle on bluff L. ◄ Continue through woods to reach road in **Althirschstein** (15km, 107m). Turn L, then bear R and immediately fork R out of village. Bear R at T-junction then turn L and continue through fields to reach road. Turn L and, after 130m, fork second R on cycle track past **Boritz** L (16km, 98m) (refreshments).

Go ahead over two crossing tracks, then turn R at T-junction and follow road to **Schänitz** (17.5km, 102m) (cycle shop). Fork R after bus stop R, following cycle track towards Elbe. Turn L then continue to reach road and turn L to beginning of **Leutewitz** (20km, 96m). Do not enter village, rather turn R on track through fields to reach T-junction. Turn R, then after 200m turn L to reach another T-junction. Turn R, then bear L and follow cycle track winding beside Elbe. Turn L beside Bootshaus to reach road (Elbstrasse) in **Riesa** (25.5km, 108m) (accommodation, refreshments, camping, tourist office, cycle shop, station).

**Riesa** (pop 30,000) is an industrial town that grew rapidly during the Communist era (population in 1981 was 52,000). The main employer is a steel works that was acquired by an Italian company in 1991 and has been completely redeveloped with modern technology and fewer employees. There is a small town centre with St Marien's church (built 1261), a Benedictine abbey, and Trinitalis church (1897). A 25m-tall 234-tonne cast-iron sculpture of an oak tree trunk is officially named after the Elbe, but is known by locals as the 'Rusty Oak'. The

*Sumo wrestlers playing musical instruments outside the Sachsen arena in Riesa*

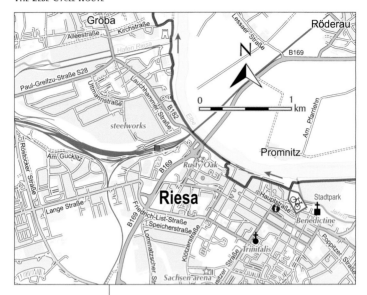

Sachsen arena is a large indoor sports hall that has held the world sumo wrestling championships (yes, really!). To commemorate this, a statue of a group of wrestlers playing musical instruments (even more strange!) stands in front of the building.

# STAGE 14
## *Riesa to Torgau*

| | |
|---|---|
| **Start** | Riesa, Elbstrasse (108m) |
| **Finish** | Torgau, Hartenfels castle (84m) |
| **Distance** | 50km |
| **Waymarking** | Elberadweg to Plotha, then D10 and Elberadweg |

Another mostly flat stage that follows quiet roads and asphalt cycle tracks through fertile country on the left bank of the Elbe, mostly away from the river. Apart from Strehla and Belgern, the villages passed are small with few facilities.

Follow Elbstrasse NW through **Riesa**, with town centre L and riverside car park R. At end, turn L uphill on cobbles (Breite Strasse) then R (Alexander-Puschkin-Platz) beside park L. Continue into Bahnhofstrasse and follow this turning R. Where road turns L around car park, continue ahead on side road that winds downhill to riverside. Just before start of cobbles, turn sharply L on riverside cycle track and continue under two bridges. Where track emerges on road, fork R, continuing on track parallel with Elbe. Turn R at T-junction then, where road turns away from river, fork R on cycle track between trees. Cross bridge over entrance to Riesa harbour and bear R to continue beside river. At next junction, turn L away from Elbe (Kirchstrasse) into **Gröba**. Turn R (Flurenstrasse), passing church L and sewage plant R. Cross flood dyke, then turn R at crossing of tracks. Pass Am Heger farm R, then fork R on cycle track through fields to **Oppitzsch** (6km, 94m) (accommodation, refreshments).

Turn L at crossroads, then bear R at T-junction and follow road past village R. Pass through flood barrier and continue to T-junction beside ferry ramp in **Strehla** (8.5km, 94m) (accommodation, youth hostel, refreshments, tourist office, cycle shop).

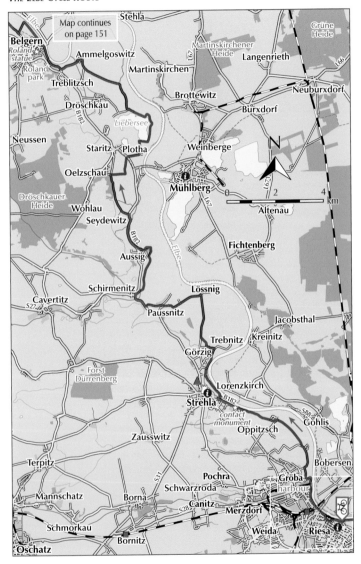

Map continues on page 151

148

## STREHLA

In medieval times, Strehla (pop 3700) was an important crossing point of the Elbe and a prosperous town. However, when the Dresden–Leipzig railway bypassed the town by crossing the river at Riesa, a long period of decline set in. As a result, there was no industrialisation and many medieval buildings have sur-

*Monument to American and Russian forces meeting opposite Strehla on 25 April 1945*

vived, particularly around the market place. The oldest part of the castle which was built to control the Elbe ford, dates from 1335, though most of the building is 16th-century Renaissance. It was owned by one family (the Pflugk family) from 1384 to 1945. In the Communist era it became a children's home, but it has been privately owned since 1994. Just after 12.00 on 25 April 1945, during the last days of the Second World War, American and Russian armies first made contact across the river at Strehla. A monument by the top of the ferry ramp commemorates the event. Torgau (30km north) also claims first contact. Although this was later in the day, the official staged picture was taken there on the following day. The actual meeting place, on the riverbank opposite Strehla, was not considered suitable for pictures as it was the site of a Russian massacre of 300 fleeing German civilians whose bodies were still on the ground.

Bear R (Riesaer Strasse), then where road bears L, turn sharply R beside house 81. Follow road winding past farm R, then continue on riverside cycle track. Bear R at junction of tracks, passing Nixstein L (refreshments, camping). Continue parallel with river to reach road and bear R ahead into **Görzig** (11km, 94m) (accommodation, refreshments).

149

Pass house with clocktower L and turn L at next junction (Görziger Strasse), then follow this winding through village. Turn R at cobbled triangular junction and continue on cycle track out of village to T-junction. Bear R, following road through fields to T-junction on edge of **Lössnig** (13.5km, 92m). Turn sharply L away from village, then follow asphalt road curving R and L into **Paussnitz** (15.5km, 95m).

Follow road winding through village, passing church R, then turn R at T-junction onto main road (Am Stein) to reach **Schirmenitz** (17km, 95m). Fork R (Schulstrasse) at crossroads in middle of village and continue past church L. Fork R over small stream and follow cycle track beside flood dyke through fields. Pass **Aussig** (accommodation) L and bear L around edge of village. Turn L at T-junction then cross small stream and turn R passing intensive pig farm L. Just before reaching main road, turn R through trees on cycle track that winds beside road. Eventually join road and continue to **Seydewitz** (21.5km, 89m).

Pass through village then turn L after house 9 and follow road through fields to crossroads. Turn R, then bear L and go ahead across main road. ◀ Continue through **Plotha** (25km, 90m) then, where road reaches active aggregates pit, turn sharply R on cycle track and follow this, circling lagoons anti-clockwise to reach **Dröschkau** (28.5km, 89m).

To visit Mühlberg (accommodation, refreshments, tourist office, cycle shop), 3km away on opposite side of Elbe, turn R beside main road then L over river bridge.

Turn L and immediately R (Brautweg) in hamlet onto cycle track between woods L and fields R. Turn L at T-junction, then fork L and R through five-way track junction. Continue through fields to crossroads just before **Ammelgosswitz** (31.5km, 88m) and turn L through flood barrier. Pass through farm, then go through flood barrier again and continue to where road bends sharply L. Turn R on cycle track and follow this winding through fields to reach ferry ramp in **Belgern** (34km, 85m) (accommodation, refreshments, camping, cycle shop).

**Belgern** (pop 4700) is also known as Rolandstadt after a 5m-tall stone statue of Roland, a medieval Carolingian/Frankish knight, that stands in the market square beside a Renaissance town hall built in 1578. In Roland park there are 14 copies of Roland statues from all over Germany. A replica Saxon post-distance column (a kind of milestone) from 1730 is also in the market square (the original is in the town museum). In front of St Bartholomew's church, a memorial stone commemorates Martin Luther's visit in 1522.

Continue past ferry house R, then fork R on cycle track through woods with open-air theatre L and pass sports ground L. Follow track round sharp bend L, then climb steeply for short distance and turn even more sharply R. Where road ends, continue ahead beside dyke R through fields. Turn L on tree-lined track into **Döbeltitz** (37.5km, 86m).

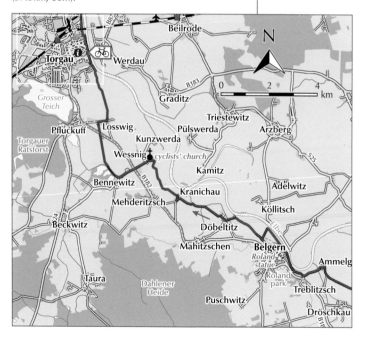

Very pretty
Lutheran church
in Wessnig calls
itself the Deutsche
Radfahrerkirche
(German cyclists'
church) and is
decorated inside
with maps and
pictures of cyclists.

Bear R in middle of village, then L at T-junction at village end. Follow quiet road winding through fields then turn very sharply R at angled crossroads into **Kranichau** (40km, 85m). Turn L in village, then continue through fields, going ahead over crossroads to reach T-junction and turn L (Linden Strasse) through **Wessnig** (42.5km, 88m). (refreshments). ◄

Go ahead over main road into **Bennewitz** (44km, 92m) (refreshments) and turn R (Am Schindrbusch) in middle of village. Continue through fields and ahead across main road into **Losswig** (46.5km, 87m). Pass church R and turn R at T-junction, using cycle track R. Turn L at crossroads (An den Linden) out of village. Go ahead R over angled crossing of tracks and bear L beside flood dyke. Cross Hafenbrücke bridge over entrance to Torgau harbour, then turn R to follow riverside cycle track under road bridge to reach schloss Hartenfels castle in **Torgau** (50km, 84m) (accommodation, refreshments, tourist office, cycle shop, station).

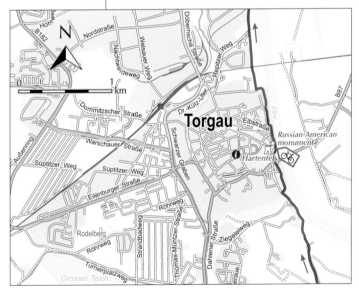

## TORGAU

*Torgau's Hartenfels castle was home to the Ernestine branch of the Dukedom of Saxony*

In 1485, when Saxony was divided between the brothers Prince Ernst and Duke Albert, Torgau (pop 20,000) became the capital of the Ernestiner territories. The prince and his successors resided in Hartenfels castle and, when Martin Luther published his theses denouncing many aspects of Catholicism in nearby Wittenberg (1517), Torgau became the political centre of the Protestant Reformation. Luther's wife is buried in St Mary's church. Hartenfels is regarded as the best-preserved early Renaissance castle in Germany. Particularly notable features include the free-standing stair tower in the inner courtyard and the Hausmannsturm watchtower at the highest point of the castle complex. The chapel was the first new-build Protestant church in the world and was consecrated in 1544 by Luther himself. The old castle moat holds a bearpit. This first held bears from 1425 to 1760, a practice that was reintroduced in the 1950s.

The rest of the town is equally stunning, with over 500 other medieval buildings in Gothic or Renaissance style. These include the Electoral Chancellery, the restored Ringenhaim house and Loebners, Germany's oldest toyshop. A more macabre modern building once held the closed youth court which directed a policy of socialist re-education for young people between 1946 and 1989. It now holds a museum documenting the repressive practices of the Communist education system.

# STAGE 15
## *Torgau to Wittenberg*

| | |
|---|---|
| **Start** | Torgau, Hartenfels castle (84m) |
| **Finish** | Wittenberg, market square (74m) |
| **Distance** | 68.5km |
| **Waymarking** | D10 and Elberadweg |

Starting on the left bank, this long stage through agricultural countryside and a series of small villages, crosses the Elbe by ferry halfway along and continues on the right bank to Wittenberg. The going is mostly on quiet roads or asphalt tracks and is almost completely flat.

*Watchtowers beside the Elbe at Torgau built to protect the Leipzig–Cottbus railway bridge*

From Elbe riverbank below Hartenfels castle in **Torgau**, follow cycle track N beside city wall R past monument to US army/Soviet army 1945 meeting. Continue beside wall R, ignoring fork R down to riverbank campervan park. Where road turns L, continue ahead on cycle track

past Altes Bootshaus L. Follow track curving L, then turn R at crossing of tracks beside flood dyke R. Pass under railway bridge, with castellated guard towers R, and bear R past industrial area L. ▶ Follow quiet road winding through **Repitz** (3km, 83m) then fork R on cycle track to follow flood dyke through fields. Bear L away from dyke, then cross short causeway and bear R beside old course of Elbe. After 200m, fork R then turn R (Torgauer Strasse) at T-junction, following road through **Döbern** (7km, 78m) (accommodation).

After house 5, turn R (Zur Alten Elbe) out of village and follow cycle track through fields. Turn L beside flood dyke, then turn sharply L at T-junction to reach Mockritz (11km, 80m). Fork L (Dorfstrasse), then pass church L and turn R (Elsniger Weg). Follow this out of village through fields then cross flood dyke and continue through woods. Bear R at road junction (road L goes over bridge to Elsnig) then turn L at next junction. Turn L at T-junction – road R

Saint Gobain and Avancis factories produce high-tech glass and solar panels for commercial and domestic power generation.

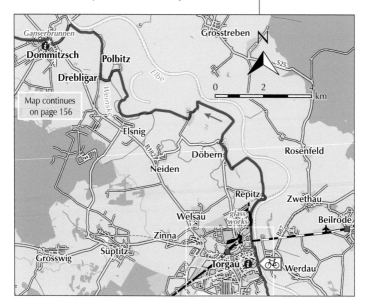

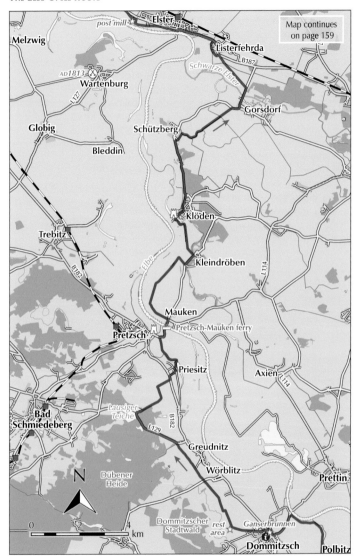

Map continues
on page 159

goes to Polbitz (accommodation) – and follow road over river Weinske into **Drebligar** (17km, 85m) (refreshments).

Turn R beside church and follow cycle track through fields. Continue beside flood dyke R, then bear L to reach T-junction (accommodation, refreshments). Turn L and follow road into **Dommitzsch** (21km, 89m) (accommodation, refreshments, camping, tourist office, cycle shop).

> **Dommitzsch** (pop 2500), also known as Gänserdommsch (goose town) as until the mid 20th century most households kept geese. Every morning around 1000 geese were shepherded down to the Elbeside meadows to graze. The Gänserbrunnen fountain in the market square recalls this activity. The nearby art nouveau town hall was built in 1911 after the old medieval town hall was destroyed by fire. Marienkirche (1493) replaced an older church plundered during the Hussite War (1429). Inside is a carved wooden relief of three saints from the previous building. The main employer is a margarine factory, but previously the town was known for the production of stoneware and pottery at the Tonwerke factory.

Turn R (Sandstrasse) before Marienkirche. At end dog-leg R and L over small stream into Dübener Strasse and follow this across disused railway and out of village. Where road turns L, continue ahead on cycle track through fields then fork R opposite cyclists' rest area. ▸ Turn L at triangular junction and follow track curving R through fields. Emerge beside old railway, then cross main road and continue past site of former Wörblitz Station. Continue to T-junction and turn L on main road. Pass through Dübener Heide forest, then turn R opposite second of two lakes at **Lausiger Teiche** (29.5km, 87m) (refreshments, camping).

Follow track through forest and fields, then bear L beside old railway line. Turn R across railway, then L at T-junction. After 150m, turn R into **Priesitz** (32.5km, 82m) (accommodation). Fork L at village green, then turn

Tree beside rest area is festooned with signs showing distances to world destinations, including Cuxhaven 666km.

*The former sailors' church in Priesitz now welcomes cyclists*

Turn L at triangular junction to reach **Pretzsch** after 350m (accommodation, refreshments, station).

R beside house 31 to reach T-junction in front of former sailors' church on banks of old course of Elbe. No longer on the navigable river, the old sailors' church is nowadays a *fischer und radler kirche* (fishermen and cyclists' church) which welcomes passing cyclists. Turn L then cross short causeway over former Elbe and fork immediately L beside old river. Cross over flood dyke then continue along tree-lined avenue. At triangular junction, turn R and follow road to **Pretzsch–Mauken ferry** (35km, 74m). ◄ Ferry operates all year 0500–1800 (weekdays), 0800–1600 (weekends and holidays).

Cross river, then pass through flood dyke to reach beginning of **Mauken**. Turn L and immediately L again, following cycle track beside flood dyke L. After 1km, fork R away from flood dyke and after a further 2.5km, follow track curving R. Turn L at crossroads to reach edge of **Kleindröben** (39.5km, 71m). Pass houses R, then opposite house 41 turn L and follow cycle track through fields. Continue, curving L and R to reach T-junction. Turn R over Kleinröbener Riss, then follow cobbled road winding through **Klöden** (42km, 76m) (accommodation, refreshments, camping).

Turn L (Schützberger Strasse) at crossroads in middle of village, then L at T-junction onto main road and follow this to **Schützberg** (45.5km, 72m) (accommodation, refreshments). At beginning of village, turn R beside house 52 and follow road bearing L through fields. Turn R at T-junction then continue through fields to next T-junction and turn R on main road into **Gorsdorf** (49km, 72m). Cross bridge over river Schwarze Elster, then after 350m fork L on cycle track into woods and continue through fields. Just before reaching main road, turn L then fork R on track beside flood dyke L, circling **Listerfehrda** R (51.5km, 72m) (accommodation). Just before main road, turn R on cycle track, then after 100m, turn L across road and L again on cycle track on opposite side parallel with road. Follow this into **Elster** (53.5km, 72m) (accommodation, refreshments, camping, cycle shop, station).

During the Napoleonic Wars, **Elster** (pop 2350) was the site of the Battle of Wartenberg (October 1813), a precursor to the Battle of Leipzig. The Silesian army crossed the Elbe at Elster and defeated a part of Napoleon's army drawn up on the opposite bank.

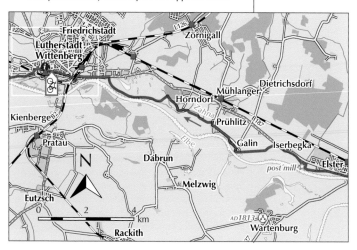

159

This began a retreat south west by the French until they were surrounded by Prussian, Austrian and Russian armies and defeated at Leipzig 16 days later. This ended Napoleon's presence in eastern Europe and forced French forces to retreat back to the Rhine.

Go ahead (Kurz Strasse) over crossroads and turn L (Gielsdorfer Strasse) at T-junction. Go ahead over main road to reach Elbe riverbank and turn R on promenade beside river L. Dog-leg L and R across ferry approach ramp and continue parallel with Elbe on Elbestrasse. Go ahead over turning circle, passing behind houses R with flood dyke L. Where road turns R, continue ahead through flood dyke on cycle track. Turn L between plinthed ferry and restored windmill on concrete block track winding through fields. Emerge on cycle track beside main road and follow this bearing L to pass **Iserbegka** R (57km, 72m). After village, turn L at T-junction and continue beside flood dyke L to **Gallin** (59.5km, 71m) (accommodation, refreshments). Go ahead over crossroads then pass Zum Schiffchen restaurant R and follow road bearing R into village. Turn L after house 10 and continue on cobbled road through village. Keep ahead at end (Schiffsmühle) to reach main road and turn L. Pass through **Prühlitz** (61km, 72m) (accommodation, station in Mühlanger). Where road turns R, fork L on cobbles and follow this bearing R. Turn L opposite house 5 and continue on cycle track through fields. Cross river Zahna and continue to T-junction. Turn L and wind through **Horndorf**. Continue past woods R then bear R through riverside meadows with Elbe R. Emerge on main road and turn L through **Elstervorstadt** (65.5km, 71m) (refreshments, cycle shop) using cycle track R. Go ahead over roundabout passing cemetery R. Turn L across road at light-controlled crossing and continue on opposite side for 50m. Turn L away from road then turn R at next junction. Turn R on cycle track under main road and railway. Emerge on road and turn L under second railway bridge. Turn L at T-junction, then go ahead over roundabout (Collegienstrasse, second exit). Pass Lutherhaus L and fork L (still Collegienstrasse) to reach Markt in centre of **Wittenberg** (68.5km, 74m) (accommodation, youth hostel, refreshments, tourist office, cycle shop, station). ▸

Collegienstrasse is pedestrian only with cycling permitted.

## WITTENBERG

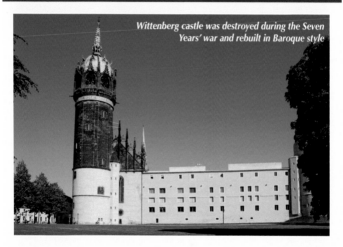

*Wittenberg castle was destroyed during the Seven Years' war and rebuilt in Baroque style*

Wittenberg (pop 46,000), officially Lutherstadt Wittenberg, came to prominence in the late 15th century when the Ernestine Elector Friedrich III of Saxony made it his residential city. He built a Renaissance castle with an ornate Schlosskirche to display his collection of relics. He started construction of city walls, which were beneficial in protecting the city during the Thirty Years' War and built a wooden bridge over the Elbe. He founded a university which encouraged the growth of printing to supply lecture texts to students.

The theologian Martin Luther moved from Erfurt to Wittenberg in 1508 and lived in the Augustinian monastery for 40 years. When the monastery was dissolved in 1525, the elector gave the building to Luther and his family and it subsequently became known as the Lutherhaus. He became professor of theology in 1512 and when he published his 95 theses attacking the practices of the Catholic church by attaching them to the door of the Schlosskirche in 1517, Luther sparked the Protestant Reformation. When Friedrich III died in 1525, his successor Johann continued support for the

161

Lutheran church, making it the official church of Saxony and encouraging its growth through other states within the Holy Roman Empire. Luther's first Protestant bible in vernacular German was published in 1534. After Luther's death in 1546, Wittenberg and its university continued as an important centre of the Reformation.

The castle and church burnt down (1760) during the Seven Years' War and were rebuilt in Baroque style. After being captured by Napoleon (1806), the city became an important military town with barracks for up to 60,000 troops. When the Prussians ousted the French (1813) and subsequently took control of Saxony, they closed the university and enhanced the military presence by turning the castle and university buildings into infantry barracks. The barracks remained in use by German and finally by Russian Soviet troops until 1992, since when they have been redeveloped as a shopping mall.

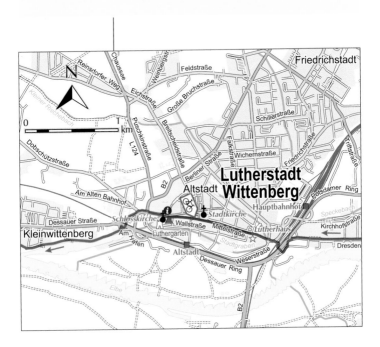

# STAGE 16
## *Wittenberg to Dessau*

| | |
|---|---|
| **Start** | Wittenberg, market square (74m) |
| **Finish** | Dessau, town hall (64m) |
| **Distance** | 39km |
| **Waymarking** | Elberadweg, D10 |

After leaving the industrial suburbs of Wittenberg, this flat stage crosses the Elbe and uses flood dykes and rural cycle tracks to cross large areas of parkland and forest, mostly created by Prince Leopold III of Anhalt-Dessau. The stage ends in the industrial city of Dessau, home to the Bauhaus architectural movement.

From Markt in centre of **Wittenberg**, follow Schlossstrasse W, passing Schlosskirche and castle L, then go ahead through Schlossplatz, using cycle track R. ▶ Continue ahead over two light-controlled crossings, still using cycle track R, then after 100m turn L across road onto cycle track beside Netto store L. Pass under railway and road bridges, then immediately turn L on short track and dog-leg L and R onto cycle track beside Wittenberg harbour L. Just before this ends, fork R over flood dyke then turn L past factory L and continue into Robert-Koch Strasse in **Kleinwittenberg** (3km, 69m) (cycle shop, station).

Turn L (Herman-Kürschner-Strasse) at crossroads to reach riverbank then turn R beside river and follow track winding through parkland. Where road turns R, fork L continuing to wind through meadows. Dog-leg over small stream then cross flood dyke. Go ahead over crossing of tracks then continue to T-junction and turn R. Turn L (Am Elbufer) at crossroads and follow road winding through housing development in **Piesteritz** (accommodation, refreshments, cycle shop, station). Emerge on main road (Dessauer Strasse) and turn L on cycle

The gardens of Schlossplatz were created on the site of fortifications pulled down in 1873.

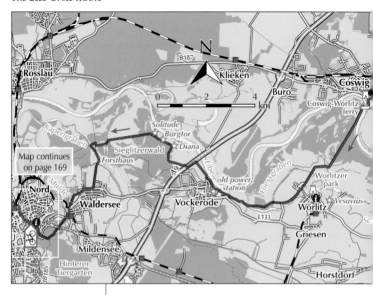

Memorial passed
R commemorates
the Elberegulierung
Griebo Nazi prison
camp for both
common criminals
and political
prisoners who were
used as slave labour
in nearby factories
from 1939–1945.

track L, passing through industrial area. Just before end of built-up area, turn L opposite PCI factory entrance on cycle track through scrubland and follow this bearing R through riverside meadows. Emerge on road in **Apollensdorf** (8.5km, 70m) and turn L (Alte Dorfstrasse). Go ahead over crossroads and where road ends at turning circle, continue ahead on cycle track through riverside meadows. ◀ Follow track turning away from river to reach T-junction and turn R (Grieboer Dorfstrasse) into **Griebo** (11.5km, 73m) (refreshments, station).

Bear L at triangular junction, then fork R opposite house 4B on gravel track passing Griebo watermill L. Follow this winding uphill through woodland to emerge beside main road and turn L. After 500m, turn L on gravel track back into woods and continue parallel with Elbe L. Emerge on road (Hasenwerder), then turn first L (Damaschkeweg). Fork L (Am Flügeldeich) at triangular junction and follow this curving R into Lindenweg. Fork L on cycle track downhill then go ahead over crossing of

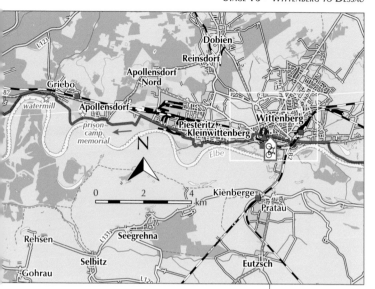

tracks and continue behind houses R with meadows L. After houses start on L, turn L and continue to T-junction (16km, 65m) with **Coswig** visible on low ridge R. ▶

> **Coswig** (12,000) grew up around an ancient castle on a low ridge overlooking the Elbe. The town and castle were destroyed (1547) during the Schmalkaldic War and the current castle, in a mix of Renaissance and Baroque styles, dates from 1677. In 1874 it became a prison which during the Nazi era held political prisoners and prisoners of war used as slave labour in armaments factories. In November 1944, 94 of these prisoners were killed by an explosion in the WASAG explosives plant.

Turn L, using cycle track L, then cross bridge over small stream and fork R. Turn L at crossing of tracks then continue through riverside meadows and bear R to reach **Coswig–Wörlitz ferry**. ▶ Cross Elbe then turn

To visit Coswig (accommodation, refreshments, tourist office, station), turn L and R, then follow series of cycle ramps up to town centre.

Ferry operates 0900–2100 (May–Sep); 0900–1800 (Apr/Oct); 1000–1700 (Mar/Nov).

To visit Wörlitz, fork L and follow road through Eichenkranz archway into town centre.

L behind hotel (accommodation, refreshments) and follow road beside river and through forest on cycle track R. Cycle track crosses to L and continues over Fliessgraben bridge. Where road bears R, continue ahead on cycle track to reach road junction on edge of **Wörlitz** (21.5km, 61m) (accommodation, refreshments, tourist office, cycle shop, station). ◀

## WÖRLITZER PARK

Wörlitzer park's iron bridge is a copy of the first iron bridge in Shropshire, England

The extensive gardens and landscaped parkland of Wörlitzer park were created (1769–1813) by Prince Leopold III of Anhalt-Dessau around the Wörlitzersee lake. The whole ensemble has a UNESCO World Heritage designation and has been extensively restored. At its centre the castle, the first neo-Classical palace in Germany, holds an considerable collection of items from the prince's grand tour of Europe, including Roman antiquities and Wedgwood porcelain. The surrounding park is dotted with decorative buildings and follies that are copies of places the prince visited on his travels. The Graue Haus was built as a retreat for the prince's wife while the synagogue (in the form of a Roman temple) and neo-Gothic parish church reflect the prince's religious tolerance. The unusual Gotische Haus has a façade modelled on Strawberry Hill mansion near London while the rear of the same building is designed as a Venetian church. Other follies include a model of the Pantheon in Rome and an Italian farmhouse. A rocky island is crowned with an artificial Vesuvius volcano that was designed to erupt and spit lava, though this no longer works. Below the volcano, Villa Hamilton is a copy of the English ambassador's house in Naples. The lake and tributaries are crossed by 17 bridges, all in different styles including a Chinese bridge, chain bridge, floating pontoon bridge and a Dutch-style bascule lifting bridge. The iron bridge is a copy of one in Coalbrookdale (England) and was the first such bridge in continental Europe. The prince intended the buildings to be open to the public, a policy which continues to the present day.

Turn R and follow cycle track beside road L. Where this ends, continue ahead on cobbled track. Fork L beside flood dyke, then at next junction fork R onto track along flood dyke, continuing to wind through woods. Pass huge brick building of disused power station L in **Vockerode** (26km, 65m) (accommodation, refreshments). Go ahead over road, still following flood dyke, then turn L just before motorway bridge over Elbe. Continue beside motorway (do not climb onto bridge) and after 500m, turn R at T-junction. Pass under motorway and continue to reach Sieglitzerwald forest. Fork R into forest, then turn L along flood dyke and pass through neo-Gothic Burgtor gateway into Sieglitzer Berg forest park.

Like Wörlitzer park, **Sieglitzer Berg** forest park was created by Leopold III of Anhalt-Dessau. Situated on a sandy ridge that raised it above the Elbe flood plain, the park incorporated existing trees with new planting and a series of architectural follies including a spa in a Greek temple, a kitchen in the form of a ruined Roman tomb, three gateways and statues of Diana and Apollo. After years of neglect, the follies have been restored to their original designs.

*Burgtor archway in Sieglitzer Berg forest park*

Pass Solitude folly (Greek temple with spa inside) and follow track winding through forest for 2km, then turn L at T-junction past Forsthaus restaurant (accommodation, refreshments). After 50m, fork R then continue winding through forest. Fork L at crossing of tracks and follow this, bearing L. Cross Kapensgraben stream and continue on quiet road (Birnbaumweg) to T-junction, then turn R (Kriesstrasse) into **Waldersee** (35km, 60m) (accommodation, refreshments, station).

Follow road bearing L then turn second R (Rotdornweg). At end, follow track bearing R and L, then continue between allotments L and football ground R. At end, turn R beside main road, crossing railway and bridge over river Jonitzer Mulde then turn immediately L into woods. Keep R at track junction and pass under road bridge. Continue winding through parkland and go ahead over crossing of tracks. Go ahead over crossroads and cycle over river Mulde on curved Tiergartenbrucke bridge. Fork R then turn L across main road at light-controlled crossing. Go through gates then pass Johannbau palace L and continue into Schlossplatz. Turn R at far side of square

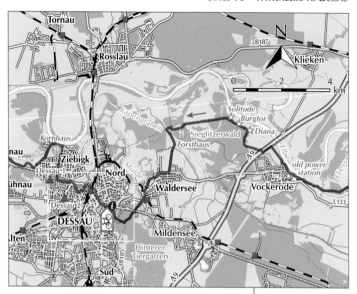

and pass Marienkirche (church) R to reach town hall in centre of **Dessau** (39km, 64m) (accommodation, youth hostel, refreshments, tourist office, cycle shop, station).

## DESSAU

Dessau (pop 77,000) was established in the 12th century as a trading post near the confluence of the Elbe and Mulde rivers. It became the residence city of the Prince of Anhalt-Dessau, who built a castle. The current castle, the Renaissance Johannbau was built in the 16th century. Badly damaged by bombing in 1945, much of the castle was pulled down by the Communist government with the west wing left as a ruined memorial. Since 1990 this wing has been restored and now holds the city museum. Industrialisation began in 1855 and Dessau grew into an important production centre. The Junkers aircraft factory attracted heavy bombing during the Second World War; the heaviest attack on 7 March 1945 by 520 planes destroyed most of the city centre. Post-war rebuilding was mostly along Communist lines and the Baroque character of the city was lost. Factories were rebuilt and by 1989 the population exceeded 100,000. After the end of Communism, many factories closed and the population declined by 25 per cent. Since then, work to redevelop the city has seen buildings renovated, industrial wastelands revived and new roads constructed.

The city is known worldwide as the centre of the Bauhaus movement between 1925 and 1932. Bauhaus was a German art school that incorporated arts and crafts into architectural design. Led successively by three outstanding architect-directors, Walter Gropius, Hannes Meyer and Ludwig Mies van der Rohe, it influenced building design worldwide. Following the pre-First World War Modernist movement, it was based on simplified forms of rationality and functionality. Bauhaus worked closely with the Vkhutemas, a similar school established in Communist Russia. This connection and left-wing beliefs of many of its adherents, led to accusations of Communist sympathies and closure under pressure from the Nazi government in 1933. In Dessau the main Bauhaus buildings include the school itself, which has been restored and listed as a UNESCO Heritage Site, and the nearby Masters' Houses, which were built as homes for the directors. Though damaged by Second World War bombing, they have now been restored. In Törten, South Dessau, the Bauhaus built an estate of 314 terraced houses. These still stand, but individual alterations have changed the look of the overall design. Later five apartment buildings (the Laubenganghausen) were added. A waymarked 17km circular cycle route connects all these Bauhaus buildings.

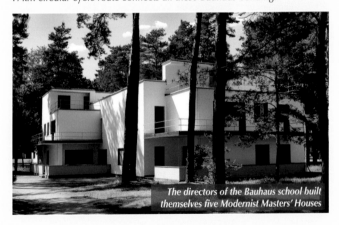

*The directors of the Bauhaus school built themselves five Modernist Masters' Houses*

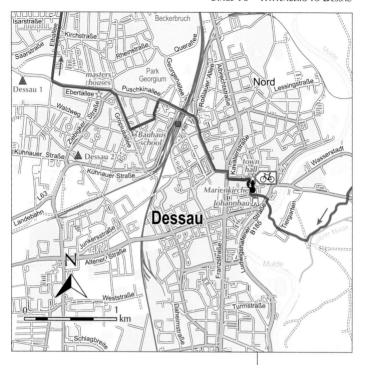

# STAGE 17
## Dessau to Barby

| | |
|---|---|
| **Start** | Dessau, town hall (64m) |
| **Finish** | Barby, Marktplatz (54m) |
| **Distance** | 41.5km |
| **Waymarking** | Elberadweg, D10 |

A mostly flat stage that leaves Dessau past the Bauhaus school then follows long stretches of forest track. The Elbe is crossed twice, by two different ferries.

From town hall in **Dessau**, follow Ratsgasse W past Rathaus centre shopping mall L. At end, turn R (Kavalierstrasse) past Bauhaus museum L, then turn L (Friedrichstrasse) at traffic lights. Fork first R (Antoinettenstrasse) using cycle track R and follow this past station L. Bear L at major road junction and continue over railway bridge. Turn third L (Kleiststrasse) to reach Seminarplatz, then bear R (Bauhausstrasse, pedestrianised) and pass under buildings of Bauhaus school. Turn R (Gropiusallee) then L at roundabout (Ebertallee, third exit), passing Bauhaus Masters' Houses L. Turn second R (Elballee) into woods and through **Ziebigk**.

The Kornhaus restaurant is a Bauhaus building designed by Carl Fieger in 1930. It reopened after restoration in 2012.

At end turn R and immediately L to reach flood dyke. Turn L past Kornhaus restaurant L (4.5km, 60m) (refreshments, camping), with Elbe R. ◄

Follow track bearing L away from Elbe, then pass sewage works R and go ahead over staggered crossing of tracks. Bear R and continue to T-junction beside obelisk L. Turn R then fork R at next junction onto gravel track winding through Kühnauerpark. Emerge on road and turn R into **Grosskühnau** (8km, 59m) (accommodation, refreshments).

Fork R and bear L, passing Evangelical church and Grosskühnau castle, both R. Fork R (Burgreinaer Strasse)

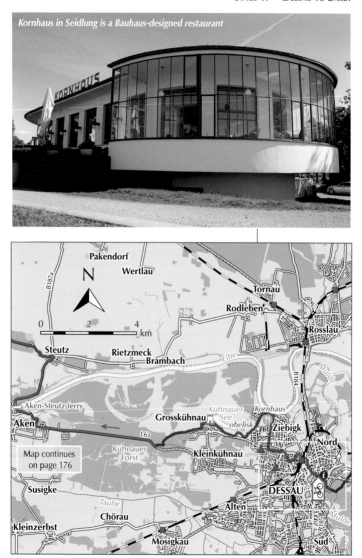

Kornhaus in Seidlung is a Bauhaus-designed restaurant

Map continues on page 176

*Passing the gates of old Friederikenburg palace in Steckby forest*

at crossroads, then go ahead through flood dyke. Turn L at next crossroads then sharply R beside flood dyke. At end of village, bear R off flood dyke with trees L and fields R and follow track winding through Kühnauer forest. Emerge on flood dyke and cross Buschgraben stream beside sluice gate. Continue winding through forest to reach main road and turn R on cycle track R of road. After 3.5km, cross to L of road and continue into beginning of Aken then turn R opposite house 24. Where road bears L, continue ahead on cycle track over disused railway then bear L on flood dyke. Turn L at T-junction, then pass small shipyard R and turn R to return to flood dyke. Continue beside Elbe and bear R on road to reach **Aken–Steutz** ferry (17.5km, 55m) (refreshments). ◄ To visit **Aken** (accommodation, refreshments, camping, cycle shop), fork L on flood dyke beside Fahrhaus restaurant then bear L over railway and turn R at T-junction (Dessauer Strasse).

*Ferry operates 0530–2000 (weekdays); 0700–2000 (Sat); 0800–2000 (Sun).*

**Aken** (pop 7700) is a small industrial town which was originally surrounded by walls built in 1335.

Only a small part of these and three gate towers still stand. The oldest buildings are the two churches: Marienkirche (1188) and Nikolaikirche. The former has been deconsecrated and is now a concert hall. The late-Gothic town hall was built in 1490 and extended in Renaissance style (1606). Industry started in the 19th century and was greatly expanded during the Second World War, with two factories producing aluminium for the Junkers aircraft works in Dessau. With other factories being established during the early Communist period, the population expanded to 15,000 by 1950. Post-Communist restructuring has seen many closures and the population has fallen by 50 per cent.

Cross Elbe by ferry and follow road to reach **Steutz** (21km, 66m) (accommodation, refreshments). Cycle uphill (Akener Strasse) to reach village centre and turn sharply L (Friedensstrasse, sp Steckby). Pass church L then turn R (Steckbyer Strasse) and follow this, forking L out of village. Soon join cycle track L and follow this to beginning of **Steckby** (25km, 61m) (accommodation, refreshments).

Turn L (Steutzer Strasse) at T-junction, passing church R, then bear R (Hauptstrasse) through village. Where road widens with trees in middle, turn R (Badetzer Strasse) beside house 22. Go ahead L over crossroads and where road ends continue ahead on cycle track into Steckby forest. Follow this for 6km, passing gates of former Friederikenburg palace, then turn L at T-junction to reach **Tochheim** (33km, 57m). ▶

At beginning of hamlet, turn R (Kämeritzer Weg) onto side road and after 100m, fork L on cycle track, continuing through forest and fields to Poleymühle. Go ahead on quiet road, then bear L at T-junction and continue to **Walternienburg** (37km, 55m) (accommodation, refreshments). Follow Hauptstrasse through village and turn L beside house 38. Cross wooden bridge over river Nuthe, then turn R in front of castle keep to reach T-junction. ▶ Turn L and follow road through **Ronney**

The entrance gates are all that is left of an early 18th-century palace now completely overgrown by forest.

Only the 14th-century keep remains of Walternienburg castle. The rest was demolished in 1988 as it had become unsafe.

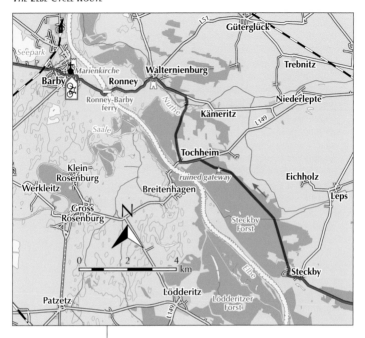

Ferry operates 0515–
2000 (weekdays);
0800–1900
(weekends/holidays).

(accommodation, refreshments) to **Ronney–Barby** ferry (39.5km, 49m). ◄

Cross Elbe by ferry and follow road ahead through fields. Pass through city walls and turn R (Breite Strasse), then follow this bearing L to Marktplatz in centre of **Barby** (41.5km, 54m) (accommodation, refreshments).

**Barby** (pop 4000) was a medieval walled town with five gate towers, parts of which are extant. The castle dates from the early 18th century. The town hall and Marienkirche church stand in Marktplatz. Post-unification population has declined from 6500 to 4000. Reflecting this, the railway station has closed and the railway bridge over the Elbe is now used only by pedestrians and cyclists.

# STAGE 18
*Barby to Magdeburg*

| | |
|---|---|
| **Start** | Barby, Marktplatz (55m) |
| **Finish** | Magdeburg, Neue Elbeterrasse (45m) |
| **Distance** | 36.5km |
| **Waymarking** | Elberadweg |

Quiet roads and field tracks are used on this level stage to reach post-industrial Schönebeck. The route then continues to the suburbs of Magdeburg and follows riverbank cycle tracks into the city centre.

From Marktplatz in **Barby**, cycle W (Magdeburger Strasse) and continue into Magdeburger Tor, then fork R (Bahnhofstrasse) beside building 22. Go ahead over crossroads and bear L (Gnadauer Strasse) and cross railway, then join cycle track R and continue through open country for 3km. ▶ Turn sharply R (sp Pömmelte) and continue on tree-lined road to T-junction. Turn L onto main road and after 200m, turn R and immediately L (Barbyer Strasse) parallel with main road. Bear R (Ernst-Thälmann-Strasse) away from main road, then fork L (Dorfstrasse) past church R in **Pömmelte** (7km, 52m) (accommodation, refreshments).

Turn R (Glinder Strasse) at crossroads and follow main road to **Glinde** (9.5km, 49m) (accommodation, refreshments). Turn L at T-junction, then fork L. Zig-zag L and R through next junction then continue out of village. Turn sharply L onto flood dyke and continue to point where flood dyke emerges beside main road at **Zackmünde** hamlet L (13.5km, 49m). Turn L and cross main road at staggered crossroads (sp Ringheiligturm). After 600m, turn R through barrier on cycle track between trees L and fields R. ▶

Old aggregates pits on right have been turned into a beach and recreation area called Seepark Barby.

To visit Pömmelte Ringheiligtum, continue ahead on road for 500m.

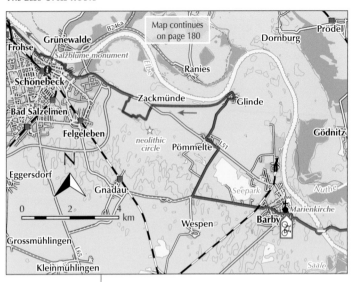

Map continues on page 180

*Ringheiligtum late Neolithic wooden circle at Pömmelte*

Discovered in 2006, **Pömmelte Ringheiligtum** is a late Neolithic circular shrine 1km south of Zackmünde. The circle has been reconstructed to show how it would have appeared over 4000 years ago. It consists of a round enclosure approximately 100m across with concentric outer rings of ditches and burial pits surrounding two inner rings of wooden posts. The whole structure aligns with biannual solstice bearings, which suggests an astronomical/religious purpose and is comparable to the English Woodhenge. In addition to human bones the outer ring of burial pits contained ceramic items, stone axes, animal bones and the remains of food offerings.

Follow track winding through woods. At end, turn R on concrete field track to reach T-junction with main road. Turn R and immediately fork L, then turn sharply back L along flood dyke beside road.

Pass roundabout L and continue on flood dyke beside main road. Fork R to go under approach road for new Elbe road bridge and pass industrial area L, still following flood dyke. Where cycle track ends, join road and after 100m, turn R after house 10A on cycle track. After 100m, fork L in front of gates and follow track winding through scrubland. Go ahead at crossing of tracks, then turn L at T-junction beside beach volley ball court and cross bridge over canal. Follow cycle track beside Elbe to reach riverboat landing stage at Salzblumenplatz in **Schönebeck** (20km, 50m) (accommodation, refreshments, tourist office, cycle shop, station).

Medieval **Schönebeck** (pop 31,000) grew up around a salt mine which continued producing until 1950. This led to other chemical industries setting up in the town. Engineering companies arrived in the 20th century and were expanded during Communist times. After reunification many of these closed, with 10,000 redundancies. As a result, population which reached 45,000 (1989) has fallen by a third.

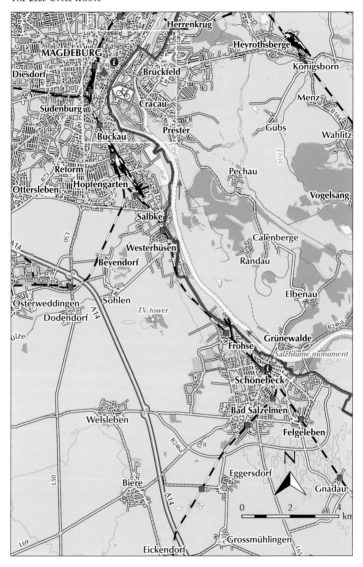

Turn L in square and leave in opposite corner (Elbstrasse). Turn first R (Müllerstrasse), then go ahead over crossroads and continue under Elbe road bridge. Where road turns L, continue ahead on cycle track and follow this curving L to reach road. Turn R (Streckenweg), on cycle track R. Where this ends, turn R on cycle track and bear L between industrial area L and riverside meadows R. Go ahead over crossing of tracks and continue past back of houses in **Frohse** L (22.5km, 48m) (accommodation, camping, station), eventually bearing L to reach road.

Turn R and cross railway, then continue to T-junction. Turn R, using cycle track R which soon crosses to L and continue to beginning of Westerhüsen. Follow track bearing L away from road then curve R beside railway L. Emerge on road (Alt Westerhüsen) and continue ahead past tram turning circle. Just before reaching main road, turn R beside Schleswiger Strasse tram stop then cross main road and turn L on cycle track. After 75m, turn sharply R downhill beside house 140 and follow gravel track curving L behind houses. Follow this to reach T-junction beside ferry ramp and turn L uphill, then bear L (Kieler Strasse) into centre of **Westerhüsen** (27.5km, 55m) (refreshments).

Turn R at crossroads (Alt Westerhüsen, with tram tracks). Pass two tram stops then turn R (Kreuzhorststrasse) beside building 65 In **Salbke** (28.5km, 52m) (refreshments, station). Turn first L (Repkowstrasse) then R (Kroppenstedter Strasse). Where asphalt ends, turn L on cycle track beside car park R. Follow this curving R and continue winding through riverside meadows beside Elbe. Bear L away from river, dog-legging L and R around *bootshaus* (boathouse) then go ahead over crossing of tracks. Bear R beside Salbke See II lake and R again past caravan park R to return to Elbe. Bear L along riverbank to reach Mückenwirt in **Buckau** (34.5km, 48m) (refreshments, station). Turn L past cafés R, then fork R under pedestrian bridge and continue beside Elbe. Where track reaches road, continue ahead on cycle track beside road and cross Klinke stream. Turn R to return to riverbank

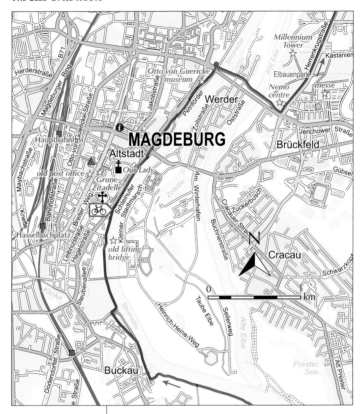

and pass under road bridge. Fork half-R over approach to former railway bridge, then continue beside river to Neue Elbeterrasse in **Magdeburg** (36.5km, 45m) (accommodation, youth hostel, refreshments, tourist office, cycle shop, station).

## MAGDEBURG

From AD968, when Holy Roman Emperor Otto the Great chose Magdeburg (pop 240,0000) as the site for his imperial palace, the city grew to become an important medieval trading centre. At the end of the 13th century it joined the Hanseatic League (an alliance of north European merchant cities) where its control of the grain trade made it the 'breadhouse of northern Europe'. This prosperity ended with the Thirty Years' War when the by then Protestant city (it converted in 1524) was captured and destroyed (1631) by Catholic League forces. Between 20,000 and 30,000 people died, the largest single massacre of the war. Post-war rebuilding saw the construction of military fortifications and barracks. When this failed to prevent capture and occupation by Napoleon (1806–1814), the defences were enhanced, making 19th-century Magdeburg the most heavily fortified city in Germany. It remained a military city until 1990, with successive occupations by Prussian, German and Russian troops.

Industrialisation in the 19th and 20th centuries saw the growth of many engineering companies. By the mid-20th century the city was the most heavily industrialised in East Germany. This concentration of industry led to heavy bombing during the Second World War, the heaviest in January 1945 destroying 90 per cent of the old city and leaving 190,000 people homeless. After the war, rebuilding concentrated on Communist-style housing

*Magdeburg's Grüne Zitadelle was designed by Friedrich Hundertwasser*

183

and industrial plants. Damaged churches were pulled down and many of the city's Baroque buildings replaced by modern concrete structures. Since 1990, reunification has seen this policy reversed. Ancient buildings have been renovated and attractive modern buildings have replaced many of the Communist structures. The main shopping street, 2km long Breite Weg, has been largely rebuilt. Particularly notable is the Grüne Zitadelle. a startling pink building designed by Friedrich Hundertwasser. Restored buildings include the town hall (1691–1698), cathedral (1209–1520), Monastery of Our Lady (1063) and old post office (1899).

Since 2010, Magdeburg has been marketed as the 'Ottostadt'. This uses two of the city's most famous sons, Otto the Great (city founder) and the scientist Otto von Guericke (who used Magdeburg hemispheres to demonstrate the power of a vacuum and became the father of vacuum technology) to promote the history, culture and industry of the city.

# STAGE 19
*Magdeburg to Rogätz*

| | |
|---|---|
| **Start** | Magdeburg, Neue Elbeterrasse (45m) |
| **Finish** | Rogätz ferry ramp (43m) |
| **Distance** | 31.5km |
| **Waymarking** | Elberadweg and D10 |

This short stage crosses the Elbe in Magdeburg then follows the river through parkland avoiding industrial areas on the opposite bank. The route crosses the Mittelland canal at Howenwarthe and follows flood dykes to Rogätz. The going is generally level.

From Neue Elbeterrasse in **Magdeburg** follow riverside cycle track N. Just before road overbridge, turn L and immediately R onto cycle track beside main road. Follow this winding through parkland and pass restaurant R (refreshments) then continue ahead on cycle track beside road R and pass Otto von Guericke museum L. ▶ Fork L under double bridge to curve up onto bridge and cross Stromelbe (branch of Elbe) on cycle track L. Continue across second bridge (over Alte Elbe branch) and pass Nemo centre L in **Bruckfeld** (3km, 48m) (refreshments).

Turn L at traffic lights, using cycle track L and pass Messe (exhibition centre) R. Continue through Elbauenpark with Jahrtausendturm (Millennium Tower) L and Seebühne open-air stage R. ▶ Pass **Herrenkrug** (4.5km, 45m) R (accommodation, refreshments, station) and go under railway bridge. Where road ends at Herrenkrug Park Hotel, bear R around turning circle, then turn R and immediately L on cycle track beside hotel grounds. Pass racecourse R, then cross flood dyke and bear L on cycle track winding through parkland to reach Elbe. Bear R beside river, passing power station on opposite bank, then follow track as it zig-zags through fields.

Otto von Guericke (1602–1686) used Magdeburg hemispheres to demonstrate the power of a vacuum.

The 60m Jahrtausendturm was built in 1999 for the Federal Horticultural Show. It is the world's tallest glued timber building and houses a museum of the history of science.

*Nemo water sports centre in Bruckfeld*

Cross Umflutehle stream and turn L at T-junction. Continue over second bridge and turn L at crossing of tracks beside Lostauer lake R. Just before **Alt Lostau** (14km, 41m) (accommodation, refreshments in Lostau 1.5km R), fork L and continue beside Elbe with wooded hillside R. Pass under motorway bridge, forking L under bridge, then after 300m fork L on riverside track with Mittelland Canal aqueduct visible ahead. Directly under aqueduct, turn sharply R uphill then after 150m turn sharply L in front of hotel back towards canal. Follow canal embankment for 250m, then turn sharply L up to canal and R along towpath past **Hohenwarthe** (17.5km, 42m) (accommodation, refreshments).

The 326km **Mitteland Canal** is the longest in Germany, joining the Rhine basin with the Elbe. Although started in 1906, the final link, the Hohenwarthe aqueduct, was not completed until 2003. Initially delayed by the Second World War, the project was cancelled when the Iron Curtain between West and East Germany closed the route between Wolfsburg and Magdeburg. It was finally completed after reunification. The aqueduct links the Mittelland Canal with the Elbe–Havel Canal and gives access to eastern Germany and Poland. Two side canals N and S connect the Mittelland with the Elbe and with Magdeburg port.

Pass under roadbridge, then bear R away from canal and continue downhill passing behind buildings at Hohenwarthe locks. At end of lock, turn L on cycle track

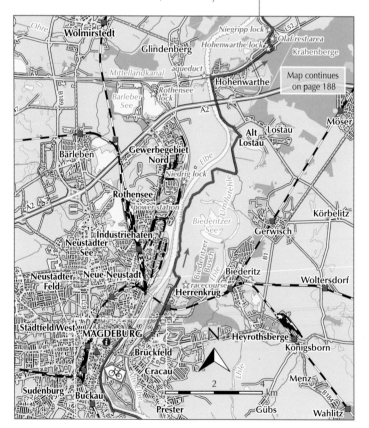

Map continues on page 188

*The cyclist rest area beside Niegripp lock is in an old barge*

across canal below lock gates. At five-way track junction, take narrow track ahead R into woods. Bear R behind houses, then turn L to reach road. Turn R, using cycle

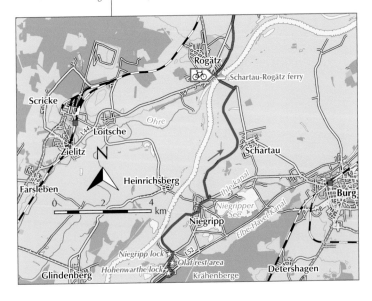

track R and continue to T-junction. Turn L and immediately R beside cyclist rest area to cross lock gates of
Niegripp lock on Elbe–Havel Canal. ▸ Turn L along towpath on flood dyke, passing junction between canal and
Elbe and bear R beside Elbe.

Bear R off flood dyke then fork L (Zum Deich) into
**Niegripp** (24.5km, 42m) (accommodation, refresh-
ments, camping). Fork R to reach T-junction, then turn L
(Hauptstrasse) and follow this through village. At end of
built-up area join short stretch of cycle track R crossing
Ihle-Kanal and turn sharply L (Zum Reiterplatz).

Fork immediately L and, after 150m, fork R on
track through fields to reach flood dyke. Follow dyke
for 3.5km, passing **Schartau** R (28km, 41m) (accommodation, refreshments) and where dyke reaches road,
turn sharply L to reach **Schartau–Rogätz ferry**. ▸ Cross
Elbe and continue up ferry approach road (Fahrdamm)
to T-junction in **Rogätz** (31.5km, 43m) (accommodation,
refreshments, station).

Cyclist rest area is
inside old canal
barge *Olaf* which
has been cut open
and installed
beside the road.

Ferry operates 0545–
2000 (weekdays);
0800–2000
(weekends). No
crossing 1145–1230.

# STAGE 20
*Rogätz to Tangermünde*

| | |
|---|---|
| **Start** | Rogätz, ferry ramp (43m) |
| **Finish** | Tangermünde town hall (45m) |
| **Distance** | 40km |
| **Waymarking** | Elberadweg and D10 |

Another level stage that uses cycle tracks along flood dykes and beside quiet roads on the left bank of the Elbe. The route passes through a series of villages perched along the edge of a low river terrace that overlooks riverside flood meadows, before reaching the unspoilt medieval town of Tangermünde.

From T-junction near ferry ramp in **Rogätz**, follow Magdeburger Strasse NE. After 75m, fork R (Steinortstrasse) through town. Where road ends, continue ahead on cycle track through fields. Fork L, following track along edge of river terrace. Emerge beside road then follow track along flood dyke bearing R and continue into forest. Go ahead over crossroads (camping) and pass La Porte hotel L (accommodation, refreshments). Continue over crossroads beside bus turning circle L and bear L to reach T-junction in **Bertingen** (8.5km, 45m) (refreshments, camping).

Turn R, using cycle track R, and follow tree-lined road to **Kehnert** (10km, 44m) (accommodation, refreshments). Turn sharply L at T-junction (August-Bevel-Strasse) and follow road through village. Rejoin cycle track R after village and continue to **Sandfurth** (14km, 45m). Continue R ahead through village to reach turning circle, then follow gravel track bearing L through trees to reach main road. Turn R, using cycle track R, and continue to **Ringfurth** (16km, 45m) (refreshments).

At end of village, join cycle track L of road and follow this through Polte (18km, 49m). After village, cross to

*A well-preserved post windmill at Grieben*

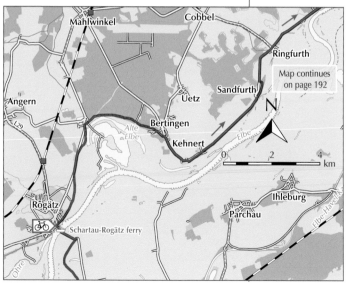

Map continues on page 192

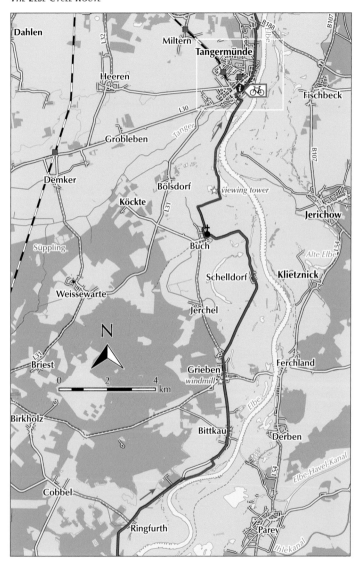

R of road, then follow cycle track winding through trees to reach flood dyke and continue parallel with Elbe. Bear L away from river, then turn R on road through **Bittkau** (22km, 41m) (accommodation, refreshments, camping). After village join cycle track beside road R and continue past windmill L in **Grieben** (25km, 40m) (accommodation, refreshments).

Bear R in village onto main road (Friedensstrasse). At end of village fork R and follow road through **Schelldorf** (29km, 35m) (accommodation). Continue beside flood dyke, eventually bearing L to **Buch** (32.5km, 35m) (accommodation, refreshments).

At beginning of village turn R (Bucher Kirchstrasse) beside church, then after village continue ahead on quiet road winding through fields. Go ahead over crossroads, then turn R on field track. At T-junction, turn L beside flood dyke and pass wildlife-viewing platform L. ▶ After 1km fork R onto flood dyke and continue to reach Tangermünde marina. Turn L, then cross river Tanger

Platform overlooks Bucher Brack-Bölsdorfer Haken Naturschutzgebiet (NSG) wetland nature reserve on opposite side of flood dyke.

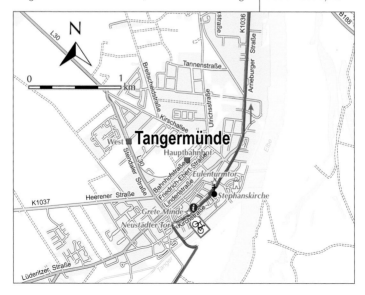

and continue ahead (Stendaler Strasse) to Neustädter Platz. Turn R (Kirchstrasse, cobbled), passing Neustädter Tor gateway L, and continue to reach town hall in **Tangermünde** (40km, 45m) (accommodation, refreshments, camping, tourist office, cycle shop, station).

## TANGERMÜNDE

*Tangermünde town hall in north German brick Gothic style*

Tangermünde (pop 10,400) is a well-preserved medieval walled town on a low rocky ridge above the Elbe flood plain. Its heyday was in the 15th century when Elector Wenzel of Brandenburg built the castle as his residence. The town hall and city gates were built at the same time in north German brick Gothic. When the town was destroyed by fire in 1617 an orphan, Grete Minde, was wrongly accused of arson and subsequently burnt at the stake. Her story was immortalised in 1879 by Prussian realist writer Theodor Fontane in his historical novel *Grete Minde*. After the fire, many new half-timbered houses were constructed, though following the Thirty Years' War (1618–1648) the town lost importance. Little touched by 19th-century industrialisation, two world wars and post-war Communist redevelopment, the medieval buildings remained intact, though slowly deteriorating. Since reunification, much of the town has been restored.

# STAGE 21
*Tangermünde to Havelberg*

| | |
|---|---|
| **Start** | Tangermünde town hall (45m) |
| **Finish** | Havelberg, Havel bridge (29m) |
| **Distance** | 36.5km |
| **Waymarking** | Elberadweg and D10 |

A stage that mostly follows the left bank using cycle tracks on flood dykes and beside quiet roads parallel with the Elbe. Towards the end it crosses the river to reach Havelberg on an island in the river Havel. Initially the route undulates gently along the river terrace but then becomes level.

From town hall in **Tangermünde**, follow Kirchstrasse NE. Turn L and immediately R (Lange Strasse) beside Stephanskirche church. Pass Eulenturm tower L and continue into Hünerdorfer Strasse. Bear R (Arneburger Strasse) at T-junction, using cycle track R, and continue past industrial area. At end of town, turn R on cycle track through fields then fork L along flood dyke and pass under road bridge. Continue beside dyke for 2.5km, soon parallel with road, then turn R on gravel road into **Hämerten** (6km, 35m) (station).

Continue ahead (Am Meilenstein) past church L, then fork R (Storkauer Weg) out of village through fields. Fork L on cycle track, passing under railway and follow this to emerge beside road and follow this road through **Storkau** (9km, 39m) (accommodation, refreshments) using cycle track R. Pass castle R and continue beside road. ▸ Eventually, fork R through **Billberge** hamlet (11km, 43m) and continue on cycle track to beginning of Arneburg. Go ahead (Tangermünder Strasse) over crossroads to reach main square in middle of **Arneburg** (16km, 56m) (accommodation, refreshments, camping, tourist office, cycle shop).

Storkau castle is nowadays a luxury hotel.

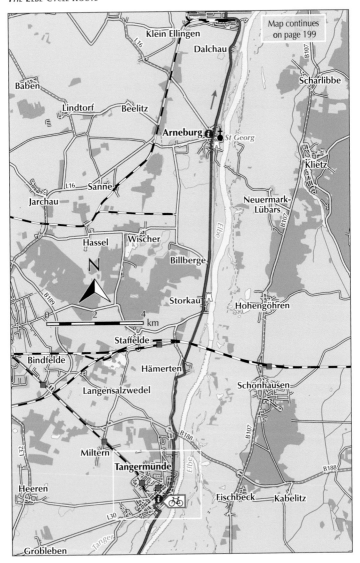

Map continues
on page 199

Klein Ellingen

Dalchau

Scharlibbe

Baben

Lindtorf

Beelitz

Arneburg *St Georg*

Klietz

Jarchau

Sanne

Neuermark-
Lübars

Hassel

Wischer

Billberge

N

Storkau

Hohengöhren

km

Staffelde

Bindfelde

Hämerten

Schönhausen

Langensalzwedel

Miltern

Tangermünde

Heeren

Fischbeck

Kabelitz

Grobleben

**Arneburg** (pop 1500) grew up around an ancient castle, built in AD925 to protect Saxony from the Slavs, which was later used as a residence by various Electors of Brandenburg. A fire in 1767 devasted the town and material for reconstruction was obtained from the castle ruins, hence only the foundations remain. Romanesque-style St Georg church, built 1200, is the oldest surviving building.

*St Georg church in Arneburg*

Cross Breite Strasse and turn R then fork immediately L (Sandauer Strasse). At end of town, pass Am Thornbeck R then turn L and R onto main road. Follow this through **Dalchau** (19.5km, 48m) then bear L beside Sofitel paper factory. Just before T-junction, turn R on cycle track and continue beside Dalchauer Strasse between partially demolished **Stendal** nuclear power station R and Zellstoff pulp mill L (22km, 38m).

Construction of **Stendal** nuclear power station began in 1982 using Russian-designed reactors similar to those at Chernobyl. Uncompleted at the time

*At Altenzaun (1806), the Prussians repulsed part of Napoleon's army during its retreat from Jena*

*Ferry operates 1 Mar–31 Oct; 0530–2130 (Mon–Sat); 0700–2130 (Sun).*

of reunification, it was abandoned in 1991 and has been partially demolished. Other factories, including a pulp mill and paper factory, now occupy part of the site.

Go ahead across side road, then bear R on cycle track away from main road. Pass cyclist rest area R and emerge beside York Strasse. After 100m, cross road to continue on cycle track along opposite side. Monument at road crossing commemorates the Battle of Altenzaun (26 October 1806) when the rearguard of the Prussian army commanded by Colonel York repulsed part of Napoleon's French army during their retreat from Jena. Where road bears R, continue ahead past **Rosenhof** hamlet R (26.5km, 29m). After 400m, follow road bearing L, then continue on road winding past abandoned Käcklitz church R. After 500m, turn R then bear R on road into **Büttnershof** (29.5km, 28m) (accommodation, refreshments, camping). Bear L past guest house, then turn R on main road and follow this over flood dyke to reach **Büttnershof–Sandau** ferry (31.5km, 26m). ◄

*Büttnershof to Sandau ferry*

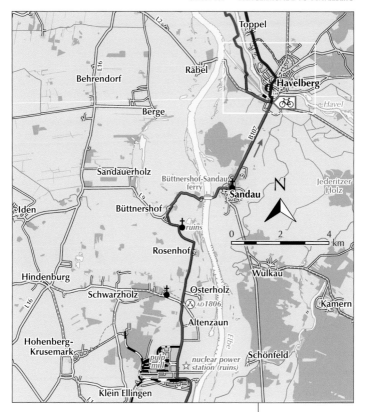

Cross Elbe by ferry then follow road ahead and cross flood dyke into **Sandau** (32.5km, 33m) (accommodation, refreshments). Turn L (Havelberger Strasse) in front of church and continue out of village. Join cycle track R of road, then continue through fields to reach end of stage before bridge over river Havel at **Havelberg** (36.5km, 29m) (accommodation, refreshments, camping, tourist office, cycle shop). ▶

To visit town centre, continue ahead over bridge.

## HAVELBERG

The first part of Havelberg (pop 6500) to develop was on a ridge overlooking a horseshoe bend in the river Havel. The Brandenburg Electors built a castle here (about AD929). Later a cathedral was built (1170) on the same location, which still stands. In the 12th century, a canal was cut across the neck of the river bend, creating an island opposite the cathedral and it was here that medieval Havelberg developed. The natural protection of the river and canal meant that only limited defensive works were necessary to protect the town, which flourished as a trading port for timber and grain at the junction of Elbe and Havel rivers. In the 20th century there was only limited industrialisation and not much Communist-era development, allowing the town to maintain its old buildings.

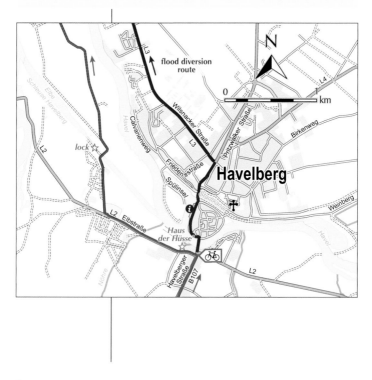

# STAGE 22

*Havelberg to Wittenberge*

| | |
|---|---|
| **Start** | Havelberg, Havel bridge (29m) |
| **Finish** | Wittenberge, Elbpromenade (24m) |
| **Distance** | 37km (39.5km flood-free alternative) |
| **Waymarking** | Elberadweg and D10 |

Saxony-Anhalt is left behind for a short, completely flat ride through the Prignitz district of Brandenburg on the Elbe's right bank. No significant towns are passed and there are limited facilities. The main route follows tracks across low-lying flood meadows which become impassable if the river is high. An alternative route from Havelberg to Gnevsdorf avoids this problem.

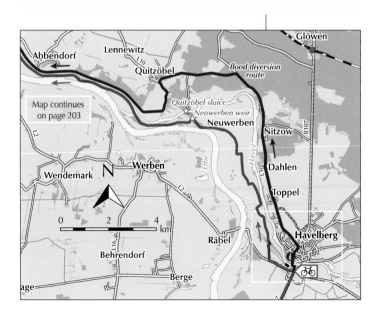

### Flood-free alternative route

Cross Havelberg bridge over river Havel and follow main road (Uferstrasse) NW through **Havelberg**. Continue over Steintorbrücke bridge across Stadtkanal and continue into Vor dem Steintor, using cycle track L. Turn L at traffic lights (Wilsnacker Strasse) using cycle track R. Pass industrial area R, where cycle track crosses to L and continue through **Toppel** (3.5km, 44m) and pass **Dahlen** hamlet. Continue through forest into **Nitzow** (6.5km, 43m) (accommodation, refreshments) where cycle track ends.

Continue on road winding through forest to **Quitzöbel** (12.5km, 27m) (accommodation, refreshments). Fork L in village (Am Brink) then follow this, bearing L and go ahead (Werbener Strasse) over angled crossroads. Bear R beside field, then bear R again along flood dyke. Follow this beside river Havel L past **Abbendorf** R (20km, 31m) (refreshments) to reach Gnevsdorfer weir. Continue past weir, rejoining main route 22km from Havelberg.

### Main route

From road junction at S end of Havel bridge in **Havelberg**, follow Elbstrasse W past Haus der Flüsse R, using cycle track R. Turn R on side road and continue over Elbe–Havel canal beside Havelberg lock. Follow concrete cycle track winding through flood meadows on spit of land between Elbe and Havel rivers for 5km, then bear R beside flood dyke. At **Neuwerben** (7.5km, 28m), climb onto flood dyke to pass hamlet and continue over bridge across Neuwerbenweir. Turn L at T-junction and follow cycle track along flood dyke, passing Abbendorf on opposite bank R, to reach Gnevsdorfer lock and weir. Turn R over river Havel and L along road on opposite bank to **Gnevsdorf** (19.5km, 25m) (accommodation).

The 325km-long **Havel** rises in NE Germany and flows through Berlin to reach the Elbe near Havelberg. It is navigable for most of its length and is an important link in Germany's inland waterway network.

*Gnevsdorf sluice controls the flow between Havel and Elbe rivers*

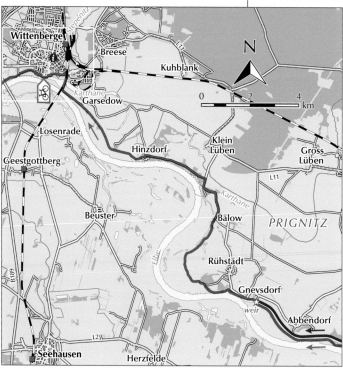

203

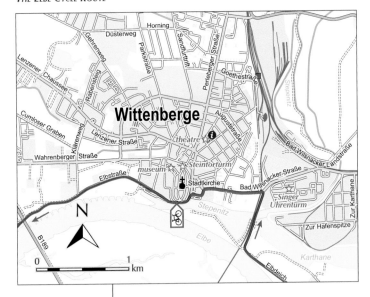

**Combined route continues**

Immediately after village, fork L onto cycle track beside flood dyke and pass confluence of Elbe and Havel rivers L. Continue beside flood dyke, eventually turning away from river to reach **Bälow** (25.5km, 26m) (accommodation, refreshments). Emerge onto road and follow road along dyke through middle of village and into open country. Pass through forest and turn L (sp Hinzdorf) on quiet road through Scharleuk hamlet to reach **Hinzdorf** (30km, 28m) (accommodation, refreshments).

Turn L in village, then sharply R opposite house 23 and go ahead past turning circle. Follow gravel track to reach flood dyke and follow this to reach road at **Garsedow** (34km, 25m) (accommodation, camping). Continue on road along flood dyke with Elbe L, then bear R beside railway and cross bridge over river Strepenitz. Turn L (Bad Wilsnacker Strasse) at T-junction and pass under railway bridge. Where road bears R, turn L (Zollstrasse) and continue into Hafenstrasse. ◀ Turn L (Elbstrasse) to reach

Zollstrasse is one-way with contra-flow cycling permitted.

end of stage at riverside Elbpromenade in **Wittenberge** (37km, 24m) (accommodation, refreshments, tourist office, cycle shop, station).

## WITTENBERGE

Wittenberge (pop 17,200) is a small post-industrial town approximately midway between Berlin and Hamburg. Late 19th- to early 20th-century industrialisation included a railway works, soap factory, chemical works and in 1903 a sewing machine factory owned by the American Singer company. This, and its employee housing estate, were designed by Walter Gropius, who later established the Bauhaus school and was the first example of his 'rationally constructed' buildings. The centrepiece was the Uhrenturm, a freestanding factory clock tower, the tallest such building in mainland Europe. This still stands and is nowadays the landmark of the city. More industry followed during the Communist era, though most of this has closed and the city's population has nearly halved from over 30,000 in 1989 to 17,000 today.

*Musically themed bronze statues line the Elbe promenade in Wittenberge*

# STAGE 23
### *Wittenberge to Dömitz*

| | |
|---|---|
| **Start** | Wittenberge, Elbpromenade (24m) |
| **Finish** | Dömitz harbour (20km) |
| **Distance** | 53km |
| **Waymarking** | Elberadweg and D10 |

A completely level stage almost entirely following the flood dyke through water meadows on the right bank of the Elbe. After Lütkenwisch, the Elbe coincides with the line of the Cold War Iron Curtain and former West Germany is visible across the river. A string of linear communities is passed, some with riverside restaurants.

From Elbpromenade in **Wittenberge**, follow Elbstrasse W. Where road forks, take cycle path between forks to join

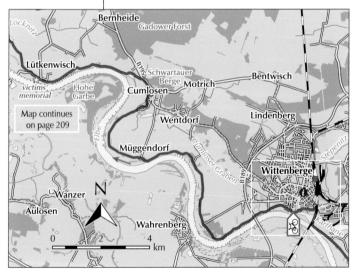

Map continues on page 209

flood dyke. Follow this out of town and pass under road bridge, then continue winding through light woodland to reach road. Cycle on this for short distance, then fork L back along flood dyke to reach **Müggendorf** (10km, 24m) (refreshments).

Follow road past village then fork L to continue along flood dyke to reach **Cumlosen** (14.5km, 24m) (accommodation, refreshments). At end of village, fork L briefly leaving flood dyke through river meadows before rejoining dyke after 600m and continuing to **Lütkenwisch** (20km, 21m) (accommodation, refreshments). ▶

A stone plaque beside the flood dyke with the inscription Grenzopfern der Elbe (1961–1989) (border victims of the Elbe) marks the point where the Iron Curtain reached the river bank.

The **Iron Curtain** was a name coined in 1945 by British Prime Minister Winston Churchill for the dividing line between the Soviet Russian-controlled countries of eastern Europe and western Europe after the end of the Second World War. It ran from Lübeck on the Baltic coast of Germany to Trieste on the Italian Mediterranean and in Germany divided the DDR from West Germany. The line was steadily enhanced with coils of barbed wire and mine fields, which the Russians claimed were to protect the Communist countries from attack but were perceived by western nations as a means of preventing emigration by the eastern populations. For 39km downstream from Lütkenwisch to Landsatz (Stage 24), the Elbe formed part of the Iron Curtain, officially called the 'Inland German Border'. A high fence and barbed wire lined the eastern bank and there were watchtowers at regular intervals. Most of this infrastructure was removed after reunification in 1989, though a few watchtowers can still be seen.

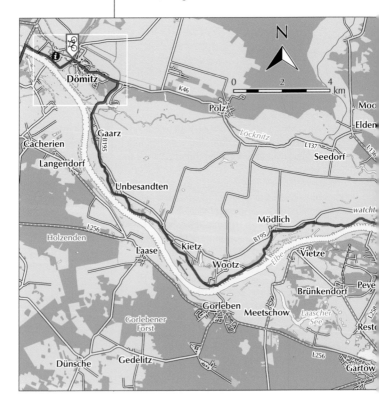

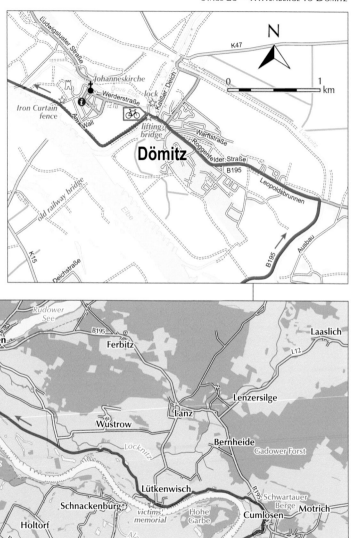

There is a preserved DDR Iron Curtain watchtower overlooking the Elbe beside Lenzen marina.

Rejoin flood dyke after hamlet then follow this winding through riverside meadows and pass Lenzen marina and ferry ramp L (31km, 20m) (refreshments). ◄ Continue to **Mödlich** (35km, 20m) (accommodation, refreshments).

Follow flood dyke past villages of **Wootz**, **Kietz**, **Unbesandten** (44.5km, 19m), (accommodation, refreshments), Besandten, Baarz and **Gaarz**. Emerge on road and turn L, then continue to T-junction. Turn L and follow main road (Leopoldsbrunnen, becoming Roggenfelder Strasse) to reach lifting bridge over Müritz–Elde canal beside harbour L in **Dömitz** (53km, 20m) (accommodation, refreshments, camping, tourist office, cycle shop).

## DÖMITZ

Dömitz (pop 3000) has two distinct parts. Altstadt, west of the harbour and the Müritz–Elde canal, has streets of half-timbered houses and a pentagonal fortress. This was built between 1559 and 1565 for the Duke of Mecklenburg to defend the south west corner of his dukedom and protect a crossing of the Elbe. It was

*Lifting bridge over the Müritz–Elde canal in Dömitz*

surrounded by bastions, casements and a moat, though this is usually dry. Nowadays the fortress houses a regional museum. East of the harbour the larger new town is occupied by residential housing and some light industry. During the Communist period, the town's position bordering the Iron Curtain between West Germany and the DDR put it in a restricted area which was closed to visitors and where there was no industrial development. The 1km-long railway bridge, which was built in 1870, was destroyed during the last few weeks of the Second World War and as it crossed the new East–West border, was never rebuilt.

# STAGE 24

*Dömitz to Bleckede*

| | |
|---|---|
| **Start** | Dömitz harbour (20km) |
| **Finish** | Bleckede, Jacobikirche (12m) |
| **Distance** | 53.5km |
| **Waymarking** | Elberadweg |

After crossing the Elbe near Dömitz, this stage enters former West Germany and follows a flood dyke to Hitzacker. Quiet roads and forest tracks take the route over a low ridge then through forested river meadows to Bleckede.

From W end of lifting bridge over Müritz–Elde canal in **Dömitz**, follow flood dyke SW beside harbour L. Bear R beside Elbe and pass Altstadt and castle, both R. Cross road serving ramp of now disused ferry and continue to reach main road. Turn L onto bridge, using cycle lane L,

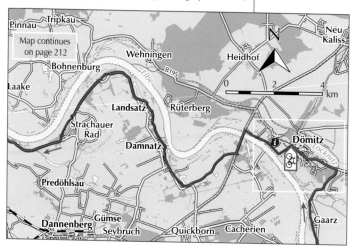

Map continues on page 212

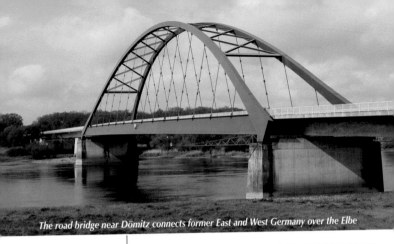

*The road bridge near Dömitz connects former East and West Germany over the Elbe*

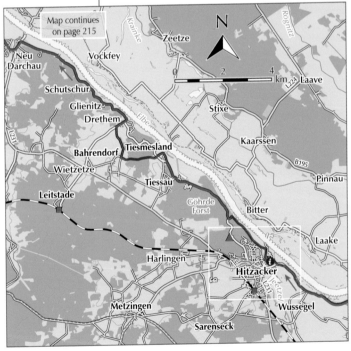

Map continues on page 215

Zeetze

Neu Darchau

Vockfey

Schutschur

Glienitz
Drethem

Bahrendorf

Wietzetze

Leitstade

Harlingen

Metzingen

Tiesmesland

Tiessau

Stixe

Kaarssen

Laave

Göhrde Forst

Bitter

Hitzacker

Sarenseck

Pinnau

Laake

Wussegel

Elbe

Krainke

Rögnitz

N

0     2     4 km

and cross Elbe. ▶ At end of bridge, turn L then L again under bridge to reach flood dyke and follow this ahead. Drop down L past Kamerun (accommodation) then rejoin flood dyke to reach **Damnatz** (8km, 17m) (accommodation, refreshments).

At end of village, drop-down L off dyke and continue beside dyke R past **Landsatz** (10.5km, 16m). Climb back onto dyke and pass Uhlenhorst L. Where road bears L away from dyke at Jasebeck and track along dyke ends, turn R through barriers on gravel track into woods. After 200m turn R beside dyke. Pass **Strachauer Rad** (15.5km, 16m), then turn sharply R over dyke and immediately L back onto dyke. Continue on dyke bearing R beside main road L. After 2km, fork L onto road and pass **Wussegel** R (18.5km, 14m) (refreshments). After hamlet, take second turn L and turn immediately R onto cycle track beside road. Just before Hitzacker, go ahead over crossroads and pass car park L, then cross dam over river Alte Jeetzel and continue ahead (Marschtorstrasse) into **Hitzacker** (21.5km, 14m) (accommodation, youth hostel, refreshments, tourist office, cycle shop, station).

Crossing the river takes the route into Niedersachsen which before reunification was part of West Germany.

*The old customs house is the oldest building in Hitzacker*

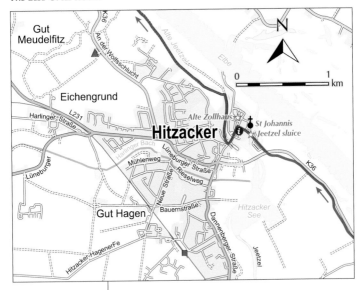

The old centre of **Hitzacker** (pop 4900) sits on an island in the river Jeetzel. There are many half-timbered buildings, the oldest being the Alte Zollhaus (old customs house), built in 1589, which houses the local museum. The Romanesque 12th-century St Johannis church, which sits beside the Alte Jeetzel, was rebuilt after much of the town was destroyed by fire in 1668. Inside it has a combined pulpit-altar, individual chairs rather than pews and a colourful set of early 20th-century stained-glass windows.

Turn L (Hauptstrasse) in town centre, then continue into Drawehnertorstrasse and cross main arm of river Jeetzel. Turn R (Am Weinberg) and follow this beside river. Where road ends beside flood gates R, pass through barrier and turn immediately L on gravel track beside Alte Jeetzel R. Continue past sewage works R and bear L to reach road. Turn R and follow road gently undulating through Göhrde forest, eventually joining cycle track L to reach **Tiessau** (27.5km, 18m) (accommodation, refreshments, camping).

Cycle through village, then continue on cycle track R of road and fork R into **Tiesmesland** (28.5km, 17m). Bear R in Tiesmesland onto road, then turn L (Triftweg) out of village. Pass under main road and continue on gravel track ascending steeply through forest for 1km to reach summit (79m). Descend to crossroads and turn R (sp Drethem) through fields. Turn R at T-junction to reach **Drethem** (32.5km, 18m) (accommodation, refreshments, camping).

Turn L in village and follow road gently undulating through **Glienitz** (33.5km, 19m) and **Schutschur** (35km, 21m). Join cycle track R and continue to Klein Kühren (36.5km, 18m) (refreshments, camping) then on to **Neu Darchau** (38.5km, 14m) (refreshments).

Turn L (Hauptstrasse) at T-junction, then bear R following road through **Katemin** (accommodation). At end

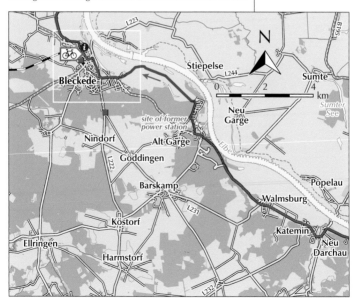

of village, join cycle track R and continue to **Walmsburg** (41.5km, 15m) (refreshments). After village rejoin cycle track R. Where road begins to ascend, fork R through barrier on cycle track into **Alt Garge** (46km, 15m) (accommodation, refreshments).

Fork R (Hauptstrasse) and follow this bearing L, then after 300m, turn R (Am Horster Felde) across old railway. ◀ Continue to T-junction and turn R (Stiepelser Strasse). Fork L over flood dyke, then turn L and follow gravel track winding across riverside meadows. Cross flood dyke, then turn R at T-junction (Wendischthuner Strasse). Opposite Renault garage L, fork R (Am Hafen) beside flood dyke R with old railway L. Fork L across railway (Am Sanddeich) and continue to T-junction. Turn L (another Am Hafen) and L again (Elbstrasse) at next T-junction. Turn R at roundabout (Breite Strasse, first exit) and continue to road junction in front of Jacobikirche in **Bleckede** (53.5km, 12m) (accommodation, refreshments, tourist office, cycle shop, station).

Open space R is the former site of a 'hidden' power station built during the Second World War using slave labour and demolished in 1988.

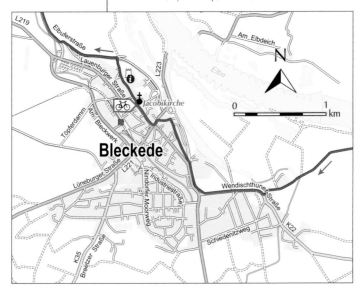

216

**Bleckede** (pop 9400) is a small town established in 1310 which was surrounded by a moat, though this was filled-in in 1929. The castle, more manor house than fortress, was built in 1600. There are a number of half-timbered houses and the 18th-century brick-built Jacobikirche. During both the First and Second World Wars, the area beside the harbour was used as a secure place to store oil reserves for the German navy in Hamburg and Cuxhaven. The 34 underground bunkers, which held 340,000 tonnes of fuel and 12km of underground pipework, were demolished in 1948.

*Jacobikirche parish church in Bleckede*

# STAGE 25
*Bleckede to Geesthacht*

| | |
|---|---|
| **Start** | Bleckede, Jacobikirche (12m) |
| **Finish** | Geesthacht, Uferpark (9m) |
| **Distance** | 40km |
| **Waymarking** | Elberadweg |

A stage which starts by using flood dykes on the left bank, then crosses to the right at Lauenburg and follows wooded slopes of a low gorge to Geesthact. Initially the going is completely flat, but becomes undulating after Lauenburg.

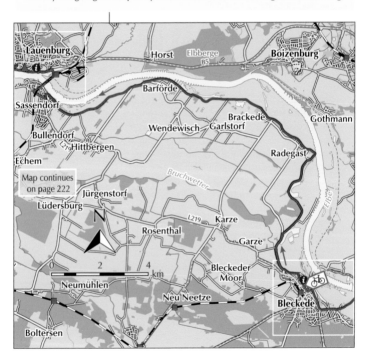

Map continues on page 222

From road junction outside Jacobikirche in **Bleckede**, follow Schlossstrasse N past castle R. Continue through riverside meadows to reach flood dyke and turn L beside dyke R. After 700m, bear R onto cycle track beside road, with flood dyke R. Where roadside cycle track ends, turn R and follow cycle track beside flood dyke R to reach **Radegast** (7.5km, 11m) (refreshments, camping).

Follow track past village, then climb onto dyke and cycle past **Brackede** (9.5km, 13m) (refreshments). Continue to Grünendeich (13.5km, 7m) (camping) and turn R to rejoin flood dyke and follow this to **Barförde** (16km, 9m). Bear R onto road and follow this through hamlet, then bear R to rejoin dyke. Continue beside dyke, following Am Deich to beginning of **Sassendorf** (20km, 10m) (accommodation, refreshments, camping).

Fork R onto dyke, with Lauenburg visible ahead, then bear L beside Fischerei museum and continue over crossroads into Dorfstrasse, using cycle track L. Cross main road at controlled crossing and turn R (An der Landesstrasse) on cycle track beside road L. Pass under railway bridge, then turn R at T-junction. Pass **Hohnstorf** L (21.5km, 7m) (refreshments, camping) and cross bridge over Elbe using cycle track L. Continue on bridge over Elbe–Lübeck canal and turn L (Hafenstrasse). Go ahead into cobbled Bahnhofstrasse, then fork L (Lösch-und Ladeplatz) along quayside in **Lauenburg** (23km, 11m) (accommodation, youth hostel, refreshments, tourist office, cycle shop, station).

## LAUENBURG

Lauenburg (pop 11,500) sits below a hillside overlooking the Elbe. In 1182, a castle was built on the hill, using stones from the ruins of Erteneburg castle at Schnakenbek (see below). Subsequent rebuilding and extension resulted in a mixture of Gothic and Renaissance styles, with a tower, separate church, bakery, brewery, residential manor house, stables and a gatehouse. Much of this was damaged by fire in 1616 and after further damage in 1656 it became uninhabitable, being finally demolished in 1817. A few parts remain including the tower and a residential wing added in 1708. The former terraced

*Lauenburg's Palm lock at the former entrance to the Stecknitz canal is the oldest lock in Germany*

gardens now form a wild garden with a restored grotto. The castle terrace provides views over Lower Saxony.

Other historic sights include the Palm lock at the entrance to the Stecknitz canal (built 1398 making it the oldest lock in Germany) and St Mary Magdalene church. Originally built (1220) in Gothic style, the lower parts are in stone and the upper parts in brick. The neo-Gothic tower was added in 1902 and the copper spire in 1992. A restored paddle-steamer, *Kaiser Wilhelm*, operates on the river.

At T-junction, bear L (Elbstrasse) through town centre. Turn L between buildings 18 and 20 on narrow street to reach riverside and turn R beside river. Pass youth hostel in Alte Zündholzfabrik (old match factory) and rowing club boathouse (both R) then follow cycle track (Am Kuhgrund) R steeply uphill away from Elbe. Opposite swimming pool complex R, turn sharply L (sp Jugendherberge) on gravel track into woods. Fork R steeply uphill and continue through stone pillars into car park of Lauenburg youth hostel. ◀ Go diagonally L across car park and continue on gravel track. Pass sports fields R and emerge onto road. Where this ends, continue on cycle track winding

This is the second of two youth hostels in Lauenburg.

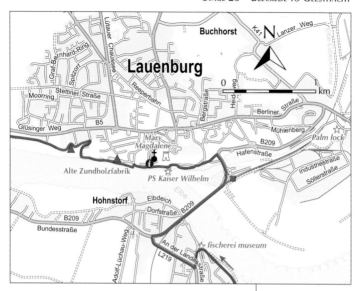

through woods. Turn L at T-junction, then bear L on road and fork R (Glüsinger Grund) through Glüsing (accommodation, refreshments). Fork L (Am Walde) and continue to T-junction in **Schnakenbek** (28km, 33m).

Below Schnakenbek (pop 850), the **ancient salt road** (Alte Salzstrasse) from Lübeck to Lüneburg crossed the Elbe by ford to Artlenburg. At the beginning of the 12th century, Ertheneburg castle was built overlooking the river to protect this crossing place. It did not last long, being destroyed in 1182 with the stones being used to build Lauenburg castle. The site became overgrown by forest and the castle was lost until 20th-century archaeological excavations led to rediscovery of the site. This same crossing point was used by British troops in the last days of the Second World War to make their first crossing of the Elbe on 29 April 1945, using amphibious tanks and armoured ferries.

221

Turn L (Alte Salzstrasse), then after 400m turn R (Sandkrug) and continue into forest on winding gravel track. After 1km, turn L following cycle path signs and follow these winding and undulating through forest. After 3.5km turn sharply L at track junction then R after 20m and continue through forest. ◄ Emerge on road and turn L (Ringweg). Follow this, bearing R to T-junction and turn L (Tesperhuder Strasse) into centre of **Tesperhude** (34km, 11m) (accommodation, refreshments).

*Left turn is easy to miss.*

Where road bears R beside Elbblick hotel, fork L on cycle track past car park R to reach riverbank and turn R on cycle track beside Elbe. After end of village, emerge beside main road and continue on cycle track L of road past **Krümmel** nuclear power station R (35.5km, 8m) (accommodation, refreshments, station).

**Krümmel nuclear power station** was built (1974–1983) on the site of a factory where in 1866 the Swedish chemist and industrialist Alfred Nobel invented dynamite. The factory grew and by 1945 it

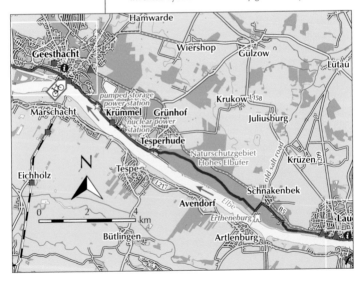

had become one of the largest explosives' factories in the world. After the Second World War, the factory was demolished and only a few of the previous 750 buildings remain.

Where road turns away from river, continue ahead on gravel track beside Elbe. Keep L at two forks, then bear R away from river past pumped storage hydroelectric power station. Turn immediately L back to riverbank and continue on riverside cycle track, dog-legging around camper-van parking place, to reach swimming pool complex L in Uferpark, **Geesthacht** (40km, 9m) (accommodation, youth hostel, refreshments, tourist office, cycle shop, station). ▶

**Geesthacht** (pop 30,000) is an industrial town on the border of Mecklenburg, Hamburg and Niedersachsen states. Industrialisation began with a glass factory in 1852 and grew rapidly after Alfred Nobel opened his dynamite factory (1866) in nearby Krümmel. After the First World War, high levels of unemployment led to radicalisation of the

*Krümmel piped storage power station works in tandem with a nearby nuclear power station*

To visit town centre (750m); turn R (Sielstrasse) across railway then continue on Markt and fork L (Schillerstrasse) opposite market square to reach pedestrianised Burgdorferstrasse.

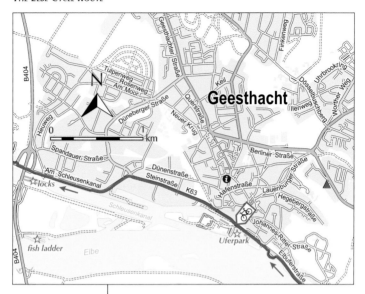

labour force. The victory of Communist candidates in local elections led to Geesthacht becoming dubbed 'Little Moscow' by the national press and street battles between Communists and Socialists, known as the 'Battle of Round Mountain', which resulted in two deaths.

# STAGE 26
*Geesthacht to Hamburg*

| | |
|---|---|
| **Start** | Geesthacht, Uferpark (9m) |
| **Finish** | Hamburg, St Pauli Landungsbrücken (6m) |
| **Distance** | 39.5km |
| **Waymarking** | Elberadweg |

A completely level stage that first follows the trackbed of a closed railway across the Vierlande, a former marshland between Geesthacht and Bergendorf where vegetables and flowers are grown for the Hamburg market. It then follows riverside cycle tracks into the centre of the city.

From entrance to Uferpark in **Geesthacht**, follow cycle track NW on L side of main road. Continue through industrial area and turn L (Wärderstrasse) at crossroads.

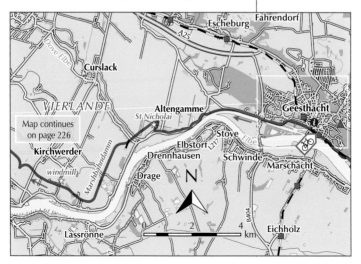

Map continues on page 226

The locks, and the weir beyond the lock island, mark the Elbe's tidal limit. Beside the weir, the longest fish ladder in Europe (550m with 45 steps) allows fish as large as sturgeon to migrate upriver.

Follow cycle track L of road and pass Geesthacht locks L. ◀ Pass under road bridge, then follow cycle track crossing to R at road junction immediately after bridge. After 1km cross back to L beside bus stop, then turn L at T-junction. After 100m, turn R across road and L on service road opposite. Follow this, winding past houses more or less parallel with main road and twice running alongside main road to reach **Altengamme** (7.5km, 7m) (accommodation, refreshments).

Turn second R (Kirchenstegel) beside house 186, and follow this zig-zagging R and L past St Nicholai church L to reach T-junction. For next 20km the route follows the trackbed of the Marschbahndamm disused railway line that closed in 1952. Turn L along old railway and continue through Achterdeich (11.5km, 4m), West-Krauel (13km, 4m), then pass Riepenburger windmill R (refreshments). ◀ Continue through Teufelsort (refreshments). At **Kirchwerder** (16km, 4m), turn sharply R and immediately fork L beside childrens' playground R on site of old railway junction. Continue following old

Riepenburger mühle is the oldest and largest remaining windmill in Hamburg.

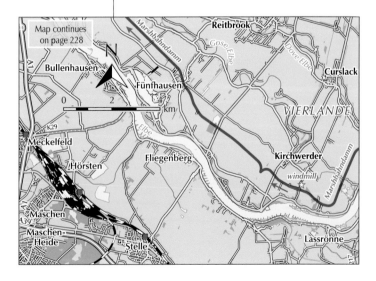

Map continues on page 228

railway past Hower See lake R to **Fünfhausen** (21km, 4m) (refreshments) beside Sandbrack lake R.

Continue through **Ochsenwerder** (26km, 4m) (accommodation, refreshments) to reach T-junction in **Tatenberg** (28.5km, 7m) (accommodation, refreshments), where route leaves old railway.

Turn L, with river Dove Elbe R then bear R (Tatenberger Weg) over sluice gates. Turn L on road (Moorfleeter Hauptdeich) and continue ahead through barriers on cycle track beside flood dyke L. Cycle under motorway bridge and pass Kaltehofe waterworks R. Continue over colourful Billwerder Bucht sperrwerk (barrage) into **Rothenburgsort** (33.5km, 8m) (accommodation, refreshments, station),

Bear L and turn L over flood dyke, then fork R beside Entenwerder Fährhaus restaurant. At end, turn L and immediately turn R on gravel track through parkland. At end, bear R over cycle bridge crossing Haken inlet, then turn sharply L to reach riverside and R pass Holiday Inn hotel R. Turn L and R to pass under Billhorner brücke

*The Italianate former office of Kaltehofe waterworks is now a museum of water*

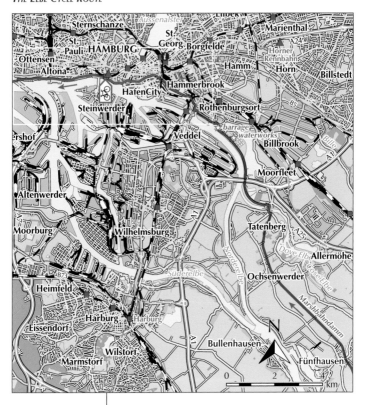

Grossmarkt is the wholesale fruit and vegetable market for Hamburg.

road bridge and continue beside river. Turn L on cycle track alongside Billhafen harbour L. Cycle under three railway bridges, then pass Brandshofer sluice R and bear L to continue along riverside. Pass Grossmarkt R and continue past Hammerbrook sluice. ◄ Go under railway and road bridges and pass Deichtor centre R. Continue following riverside cycle track past St Katharinen church and Baumwall metro station to reach ferry landing stage at St Pauli Landungsbrücken in **Hamburg** (39.5km, 6m) (accommodation, youth hostel, refreshments, tourist office, cycle shop, station).

## HAMBURG

*Hamburg waterfront*

Hamburg (pop 1,835,000), the second largest city in Germany after Berlin, grew up as a medieval trading port and member of the Hanseatic League of merchant cities. The city's boom period was from the start of German industrialisation in the mid-19th century until the First World War. During this period, much of the old medieval city was swept away and replaced with new brick buildings, while the city walls were demolished. In the west and north their course became a series of linear parks, including Planten un Blomen, while in the east it was used for the main railway station. Many medieval buildings not replaced by 19th-century development suffered from Second World War bombing, so there are very few pre-19th-century structures in the city.

Trading remains important, with Hamburg being the third biggest port in Europe by tonnage handled. The nature of trade has changed, however, with large container ships using facilities downriver from the centre. The city centre docks have closed to shipping and are in the process of redevelopment into commercial, residential and entertainment areas. The Speicherstadt free-port district of brick-built warehouses, which was constructed between 1883 and 1927 on two islands just south of the Altstadt, is being redeveloped as part of HafenCity, while the Kontorhausviertel quarter of large office

buildings for shipping companies in early 20th-century brick expression-
ist style is being renovated. Both these areas are listed as UNESCO World
Heritage Sites. Other important buildings include the city hall and five main
churches. Other churches were destroyed by Second World War bombing including St Nikolai. Its 147m-tall ruined spire, the tallest in the city
and for a short period (1874–1877) tallest in the world, has been preserved
as a memorial to victims of the war and tyranny. The Elbe and Alster flow
through the city in a variety of channels, connected by canals with many
waterfronts lined with brick-built façades.

The most obvious landmark is the Heinrich-Hertz-Turm. This 279m-high
tower broadcasts radio and TV programmes to the city. Originally it had a
public restaurant and viewing platform but this closed during renovation
in 1961 to remove asbestos cladding and did not reopen after the opera-
tors found that the cost of restoring the public areas and equipping them
to new higher safety standards was unaffordable. The Elbphilharmonie is a
modern part-brick/part-concrete concert hall that rises over the harbour. In
St Pauli district, the Reeperbahn is the main nightlife street, lined with restaurants, nightclubs, discotheques, bars, strip clubs, sex shops and brothels.

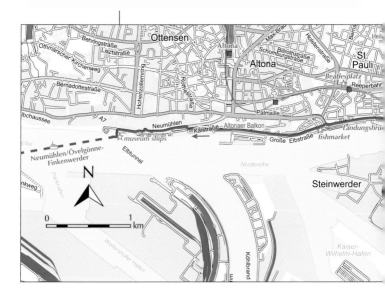

*Chrome statues in Beatlesplatz mark the group's early years performing in Reeperbahn clubs*

It was here that on 17 August 1960 The Beatles played their first performance (they had played before in Liverpool as The Quarrymen) and went on to play over 250 performances in various Reeperbahn clubs. John Lennon was later quoted saying he was 'born in Liverpool, but made in Hamburg'.

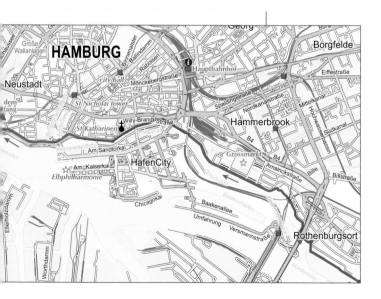

# STAGE 27
*Hamburg to Stade*

| | |
|---|---|
| **Start** | Hamburg, St Pauli Landungsbrücken (6m) |
| **Finish** | Stade, Beim Salztor bridge (6m) |
| **Distance** | 42km (plus 3km ferry) |
| **Waymarking** | Elberadweg |

After using a ferry to cross the Elbe beside Hamburg harbour, this completely flat stage soon leaves the city's suburbs, using cycle tracks beside main roads and along flood dykes to cross the Altes Land, an area of drained former marshland on the left bank of the river.

Map continues
on page 234

From St Pauli Landungsbrücken in **Hamburg**, follow St Pauli Hafenstrasse W, using cycle track R. Where this turns R away from riverside, fork L (Grosse Elbstrasse) through fishmarket area, continuing parallel with river.

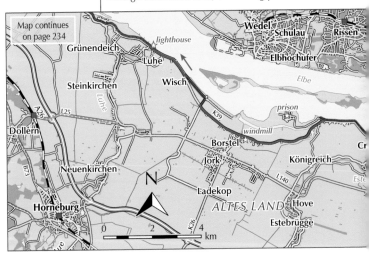

Map continues
on page 234

*A frequent waterbus service links piers along Hamburg's waterfront*

Where road ends, bear R away from Elbe then turn immediately L (Neumühlen) with Heine Park R. Continue to reach **Neumühlen/Övelgönne** pier beside museum ship harbour L (4km, 0m) and take waterbus Route 62 to **Finkenwerder** pier (7km, 0m) (accommodation, refreshments, cycle shop). ▶

Waterbus 62 runs every 15min; 0515–2345 all year. Disembark at second port of call.

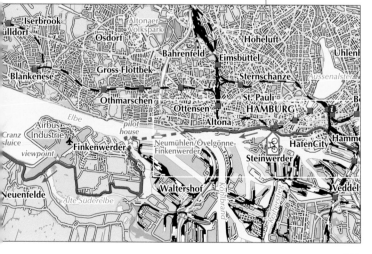

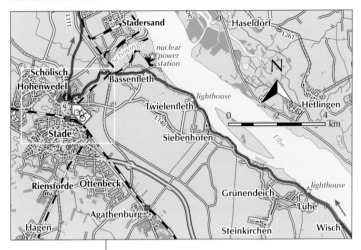

**Finkenwerder** (pop 11,750) sits on an island between two arms of the Elbe. The pretty former fishing village on the north side of the island, where the ferry arrives, has been surrounded by suburban accommodation and a vast factory for Airbus Industrie with its own airfield.

Turn L (Benittstrasse) at end of ferry ramp then go ahead at first junction and follow road bearing R to reach roundabout. Turn L (Köhlfleet Hauptdeich, third exit), then turn second R (Kanalstack). Fork L (Sandhöhe) then fork L again (Auedeich) beside house 23. Fork R (still Auedeich) after house 70, then, where road bears R, turn L after house 107 and immediately R on cycle track beside flood dyke (Aue-Hauptdeich). Where this ends, turn sharply R beside road and immediately L (Osterfelddeich). Follow this, bearing R, then turn L (Bodemannweg). Turn L (Süderkirchenweg) at T-junction then continue into Finkenwerder Süderdeich and follow road bearing R beside river Alte Süderelbe. Bear R again, then emerge on Finkenwerder Westerdeich and continue ahead. Where this bears R, fork L on cycle track beside car park.

Turn L at T-junction of tracks to reach main road and turn L (Nessdeich) using cycle track R. Continue beside Finkenwerder airfield R and pass viewing terrace R. ▶

> The area between Neuenfelde and Stade is known as the **Altes Land**. Originally marshland, it was drained by Dutch engineers in the 12th century and surrounded by flood dykes and pumping windmills. Nowadays this fertile soil is Germany's largest fruit-producing area with orchards of apple, cherry, pear and plum trees stretching from horizon to horizon. Longitudinal villages of half-timbered red-brick houses and barns with thatched roofs are reminiscent of Holland.

Bear R at T-junction then follow main road round end of runway and past entrance to Airbus factory R. Continue past turn-off L for **Neuenfelde** (17km, 4m) (accommodation, refreshments) to reach lifting bridge and sluice gates at **Cranz** schleuse (18km, 6m) (accommodation, refreshments). Immediately after bridge, turn sharply R downhill back towards bridge then fork sharply L beside flood

Airbus Industrie produce Airbus A320, A330, A350 and A380 aircraft at Finkenwerder. The runway is used to test new planes and fly in parts from other factories in giant Beluga transport aircraft.

*The reclaimed Altes Land is extensively planted with fruit orchards*

*Twielenfleth lighthouse stands on the Elbe flood dyke*

*Security fence is for Hahnofersand young offenders' prison on an island in the Elbe.*

dyke. Where this ends at security fence, turn sharply L to reach main road and R beside main road, using cycle track L. ◀ Follow this through **Borstel** (26km, 2m) (accommodation, refreshments, plus cycle shop in Jork, 2km), passing Jork preserved windmill L, to Neuenschleuse (28km, 2m) (accommodation, refreshments).

Pass turn on L (sp Mittelnkirchen) and immediately turn R (Yachthafenstrasse) beside fire station. At end turn L beside flood dyke and continue to **Wisch** (30km, 2m) (accommodation, refreshments). Emerge on main road and turn R using cycle track L, then continue to **Lühe** (31.5km, 2m) (accommodation, refreshments). Cross lifting bridge over river Lühe and pass lighthouse R, then turn R across main road (sp Personenfähre), and through flood dyke. Turn L beside car park on cycle track between flood dyke L and Elbe R. Continue past **Grünendeich** (34km, 3m) (accommodation, refreshments, cycle shop) to **Twielenfleth** (38km, 8m) (refreshments, cycle shop).

Pass black and white lighthouse L, then take second fork L over flood dyke. Bear R on main road, using cycle track L, then turn L at crossroads into **Bassenfleth** (41km, 2m). ▸ Follow cycle track switching to R, then turn R (Am Wegen, sp Melau) through village and continue through Melau. Cross railway and pass under road bridge. Bear L (Am Schwingendeich) at road junction and continue beside river Schwinge R into beginning of Stade. Turn sharply R (sp Schiesssportanlage) onto flood dyke then fork L and follow this bearing L on gravel track beside canal R. Bear R again then turn L along quayside of Stade harbour and continue with harbour R to sluice gate. Turn R over Beim Salztor bridge into **Stade** (45km, 6m) (accommodation, youth hostel, refreshments, tourist office, cycle shop, station).

Road on right at crossroads leads to decommissioned Stade nuclear power station which closed in 2003.

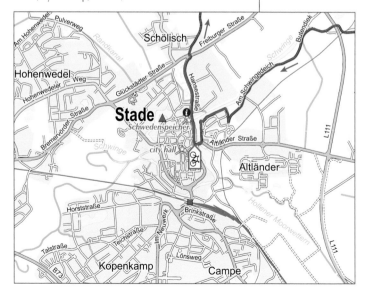

## STADE

*The old harbour in Stade was once an important Hanseatic League port*

The old centre of Stade (pop 47,500) sits on Schwingeinsel, an island formed by a moat cut across the apex of a horseshoe loop in the river Schwinge. Newer (and larger) parts of the city have developed outside this loop, particularly to the south and west. Two elements shaped the old city. In 1373 Stade joined the Hanseatic League and remained a member until 1601 when it was expelled for forming an alliance with the Merchant Adventurers, an English trading company that was a fierce rival of the League. During this period the harbour developed as a trading port and the link to the Elbe via the Schwinge was deepened and straightened. Most of the medieval buildings from this period were destroyed by fire in 1659, but some buildings and two churches remain. The city hall was destroyed, but its vaults survived and the Ratskeller tavern in the vaults, which first opened 1305, is one of the oldest in Germany. In 1643, Swedish forces captured Stade and it remained in Swedish hands until 1712. Post-fire rebuilding was done by the Swedes and many of the buildings in the old town date from this period, including whole streets of half-timbered houses. Of particular note, the Schwedenspeicher (1705) is a Baroque-style brick-built provisioning warehouse which nowadays houses the city museum.

## STAGE 28

*Stade to Freiburg*

| | |
|---|---|
| **Start** | Stade, Beim Salztor bridge (6m) |
| **Finish** | Freiburg, Am Hafen quayside (7m) |
| **Distance** | 41.5km (31.5km via direct route) |
| **Waymarking** | Elberadweg |

A completely flat stage that winds across fertile farmland of Kehdingen, mostly away from the Elbe. The route follows quiet roads or runs beside flood dykes passing a string of small communities and farms. An alternative direct route, which closely follows the main Elbe flood dyke, is only passable during limited weekend hours.

From W side of Beim Salztor bridge over river Schwinge in **Stade**, follow Hansestrasse N beside harbour, using cycle track R. Cross bridge over entrance to Alter Hafen and continue to roundabout in **Schölish** (accommodation, refreshments).

Go ahead over roundabout (second exit) onto road passing cemetery R. After 60m, keep ahead on short

*The cycle route follows flood dykes across the salt marshes of Kehdingen*

gravel track to reach road (Schneeweg) and follow this into open country. Pass Schnee hamlet R, then cross main road and follow cycle track beside dyke R. Cross another road, continuing beside dyke, now with houses beside track. Fork R, then emerge on road and bear L into **Bützfleth** (6km, 2m) (accommodation).

Turn R at roundabout (Obstmarschenweg, first exit), following cycle track R, then R again at second roundabout (Deichstrasse, first exit) on road beside dyke R.

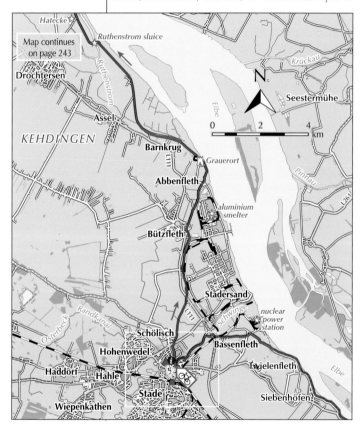

Map continues
on page 243

240

Follow this through **Abbenfleth** (8km, 5m) and continue (Elbstrasse) past festung Grauerort fort L.

> **Grauerort fort** was built in 1869 as part of a defensive shield for Hamburg during the Franco-Prussian War (1870–1871). It never saw action and after the First World War was converted to a naval mine arsenal with a 250m-long pier for receiving and despatching mines. After it closed in 1985, the fort remained unused until 1997 as large amounts of toxic chemicals had to be removed before it could be restored and reopened as a museum. After the Second World War, the pier held an unusual restaurant called Klein Heligoland ('Little Heligoland'). This developed when Heligoland island in the North Sea, a popular pre-war day-trip destination from Hamburg, was closed to visitors for military reasons. Cruise boats came instead to Little Heligoland.

Cycle through **Barnkrug** (10.5km, 5m) on Am Elbdeich and continue following dyke through fields to

*In the 1950s Grauerort pier was 'Little Heligoland' for boat excursions from Hamburg*

241

Hatecke produce fibreglass boats, particularly lifeboats.

cross sluice over river Ruthenstrom. By Hatecke factory, dog-leg R and L through gap in flood dyke. ◄ After 900m take middle of three tracks ahead, then emerge on road and continue to **Krautsand** (21km, 4m) (accommodation, refreshments, camping, cycle shop).

From Krautsand to Freiburg there is a choice of routes. The direct route (10km shorter) which crosses the Wischhafener Süderelbe sluice, is only passable at weekends and on holidays 1000–1200 and 1700–19.00 when the lifting bridge over the sluice is lowered to provide access. At all other times it is necessary to follow the main route described via Dornbusch.

**Direct route (limited hours on Sat/Sun and holidays only)**
Go straight ahead, then fork R to continue beside flood dyke R, passing through a series of gates. After 4.75km, cross lifting bridge over **Wischhafener Süderelbe** flood barrier. Turn L at main road, using cycle track R, then after 150m turn sharply R to rejoin main route beside flood dyke.

**Main route**
Turn L (Elbstrasse), then R (Krautsander Strasse) at T-junction. At end of town, join cycle track beside road L and follow this to **Dornbusch** (24.5km, 1m) (refreshments, cycle shop). Cross lifting bridge and pass through flood dyke, then turn sharply L (Alter Weg) beside building 65. Turn R (Fohlenstrasse) then go ahead over main road into Hüller Strasse, sp Hüll) and follow this out of village using cycle track R. Continue to T-junction and turn R (Dornbuschermoor), using cycle track R. When cycle track ends continue on road through **Wolfsbruch** then go ahead over crossroads (accommodation, refreshments) through Neulandermoor (29.5km, 2m) using cycle track R. After 2.5km, turn L (Moorchaussee, sp Wischhafen) and follow road, initially on cycle track R then switching to L, into **Wischhafen** (33.5km, 3m) (accommodation, refreshments, tourist office, cycle shop).
Bear L at T-junction, still on cycle lane L, cycling through village to reach road junction at end of village.

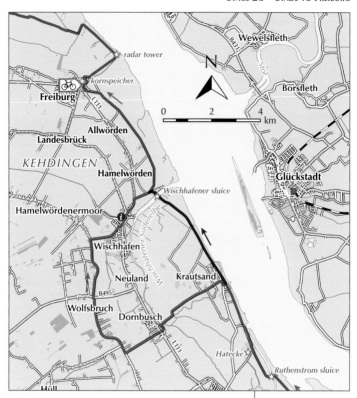

Turn R (Glückstädter Strasse, sp Glückstadt) then, where road crosses flood dyke, fork L on cycle track beside dyke.

**Combined route continues**
Follow cycle track beside flood dyke R through series of gates, then emerge on road (Allwördener Deich. Pass wildlife viewing tower R and continue to the beginning of Freiburg. Turn sharply R (Öbern Diek) over dyke, then sharply L to reach quayside (Am Hafen) in centre of **Freiburg** (41.5km, 7m) (accommodation, refreshments). ▶

Freiburg is a small town (pop 1850) with a harbour linked by a narrow canal with the Elbe. In the village centre, the *historischer kornspeicher* (old granary) is now a cultural centre.

243

# STAGE 29
*Freiburg to Cuxhaven*

| | |
|---|---|
| **Start** | Freiburg, Am Hafen quayside (7m) |
| **Finish** | Cuxhaven, Kapitän-Alexander-Strasse (4m) |
| **Distance** | 51.5km (+4.5km to Kugelbake point) |
| **Waymarking** | Elberadweg |

Completely flat, this last stage continues across the wide flood plain and salt marshes of Kehdingen that line the Elbe estuary. It mostly follows cycle tracks beside either flood dykes or drainage canals before ending in the industrial port of Cuxhaven, from where a short excursion takes you to the mouth of the river at Kugelbake.

Follow Am Hafen NE beside **Freiburg** harbour, passing old brick and half-timbered *kornspeicher* granary L. Turn L (Neue Strasse) beside fire station R then go

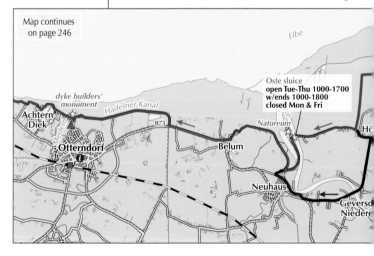

Map continues
on page 246

ahead over crossroads and turn R (Dampferstieg) out of town. Continue to T-junction and turn L beside dyke. Follow this past radar tower R, bearing L beside estuary. By next (small) sluice, fork L over dyke and follow track (Schöneworther Weg) away from estuary. Bear R beside drainage canal, then dog-leg L and R (Sommerdeichstrasse), continuing between fields. Dog-leg L and R again at next track junction then continue through fields for 11km. At fourth crossing of tracks, turn L (Gellertweg) and cross small drainage canal. At T-junction, turn L climbing over dyke into **Hörne** (20.5km, 4m) (accommodation, refreshments).

At Hörne there is a choice of routes. The main route crosses the river Oste over the Ostesperrwerk sluice with limited crossing times (all year Tue–Thu 1000–1700; weekends Apr–Sep 1000–1800, Oct–Mar 1000–1700). At other times, including all day Mon and Fri, an alternative route via Neuhaus (2.5km longer) must be taken.

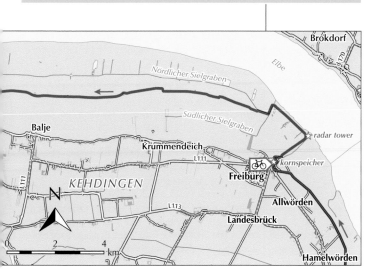

245

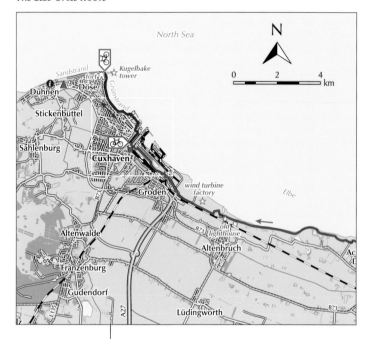

### Alternative route

Go ahead through Hörne to reach T-junction. Turn R and continue out of village, soon joining cycle track L. Cross river Oste and continue to point 50m before T-junction with main road. Fork R and follow road through **Neuhaus**. Fork R (Schulplatz) in village and continue into Deichstrasse. At end of village, turn R (Neuhäuser Deich) and after 250m fork L (sp Belum) to rejoin main route.

### Main route via Oste sluice

Turn sharply R (Aussendeich) beside dyke, then go ahead to reach river Oste (23km, 8m). Cross **Oste sluice** and turn L, passing car park R, then L again at T-junction on road along dyke beside Oste. At point where road crosses another flood dyke, turn sharply second R (Neuhäuser Deich, sp Belum) alongside dyke R. ◀

First turn right runs below wrong side of dyke.

**Combined route continues**

Continue through Neuhäuser Deich (26km, 3m). Eventually follow road bearing L away from dyke and winding through **Belum** (29.5km, 4m) (cycle shop) to reach T-junction.

Turn R on main road using cycle track R and continue for 2.5km, then turn R beside Hadelner Kanal. Follow this bearing L to cross canal at **Otterndorf** schleuse (36km, 8m) (accommodation, refreshments, youth hostel; plus tourist office, cycle shop, station in Otterndorf 2km off route).

Continue ahead (Prof Carl-Langhein-Weg), then just before next canal bridge turn sharply R (Schleuse) and continue over two sluice gates across river Medem. Fork immediately L (Deichstrasse) on road below flood dyke R and follow this winding past caravan park and holiday home development at **Achtern Diek** (38km, 3m) (refreshments, camping). Where gate blocks way ahead, turn L on cycle track winding through campsite. Turn R at road crossing, then R again at T-junction and bear L beside flood dyke. Follow track away briefly from dyke passing small lagoon R, then continue below dyke. Opposite Otterndorf youth summer camp L, fork R through gate

*The old Dicke Berta lighthouse at Altenbruch has been preserved*

climbing over dyke and bear L briefly beside estuary then continue on track for 4.5km, now with dyke L. Pass black and white light tower R and campsite above dyke L, then fork L past Dicke Berta preserved lighthouse L to reach sluices at **Altenbruch** schleuse (45.5km, 6m) (accommodation, refreshments, camping).

Dog-leg L and R to continue beside dyke, then turn L past Rozhledna viewing tower L. Follow track bearing R and pass Siemens wind turbine assembly plant R. Emerge on road and continue ahead, using cycle track R, over next two junctions, then cross railway and continue ahead at next road junction. Where cycle lane ends, continue ahead on road (Neufelder Strasse) through industrial area. Bear L past fishermen's museum R, then bear R and L to reach T-junction with Kapitän-Alexander-Strasse in **Cuxhaven** (51.5km, 5m) (accommodation, refreshments, cycle shop, station; plus youth hostel, camping, tourist office in Dühnen).

## CUXHAVEN

Cuxhaven (pop 48,500) is two towns in one: a workmanlike port and fishing harbour and an elegant seaside resort at the mouth of the Elbe. The first visitors arrived in 1816 and wide sand beaches along the North Sea coast have been attracting holidaymakers ever since; three million overnight stays make it one of the busiest coastal resorts in Germany. Most hotels and resort facilities are in Döse and Dühnen which stretch along the coast north west of the main town. In the centre, the 10-storey red-brick *wasserturm* (water tower) with green copper spire dominates the townscape. No longer needed to maintain water pressure, it is now privately owned. The harbour is a busy fishing port for both deep-sea trawlers and inshore shrimp cutters. From 1889 to 1972, it was a major point of embarkation for transatlantic liners and a route by which many Germans emigrated to the US. The former Hapag-Hallen (ocean terminal building) has been renovated and now serves as a disembarkation point for cruise ship passengers. Since 1997 major developments include the building of Cuxport, a new deep-water port with ro-ro facilities for vehicle shipping and container handling infrastructure. Nearby two plants are involved in the construction and shipment of off-shore wind turbines.

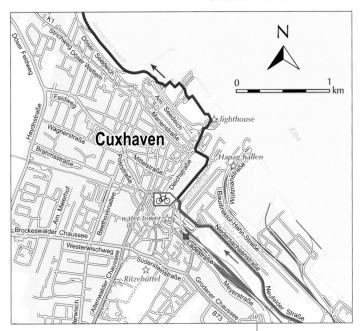

### Excursion to Elbe mouth at Kugelbake

Turn R (Kapitän-Alexander-Strasse), then follow this bearing L (Zollkaje) over Klappbrucke lifting bridge. Bear R at T-junction (Am Alten Hafen), then go through flood gates and pass quayside R. Fork R, then continue ahead towards red-brick lighthouse. Turn L in front of lighthouse, then fork immediately R over grassy bank to reach harbourside. Turn L past yacht haven R, then bear L away from quayside to circle yacht club. Emerge onto road and after 100m turn L past camper-van park R. Follow blue line painted on road to cross three large car parks then turn R and continue on cycle track beside Grünstrand beach. Pass Kugelbakefort L to reach Sandstrand beach. ▶ Elbe cycleway ends here. Last 300m along sandy spit to **Kugelbake** tower (5km from Cuxhaven, 0m) must be done on foot.

Kugelbake fort was a coastal battery of 14 guns built just before the Franco-Prussian War (1870–1871) to defend Hamburg and the Elbe from naval attack.

*The Elbe cycle route ends at a marker on the cycle track above Sandstand beach*

The **Kugelbake** is a 28m-high wooden navigational mast at the mouth of the Elbe (18km wide at this point), which since 1913 has been the official symbol of Cuxhaven and appears on the coat of arms. The first mast was built in 1703. This was made of wood, as were all its successors, making renewal necessary every 30 years. During one of these restorations in 1853 it was fitted with a light. Nowadays it has no maritime role, with all shipping being guided by radio, radar and GPS signals. However, it is still illuminated at night as a tourist attraction.

Congratulations, you have reached the end of your ride and it is now time to return home. To reach Cuxhaven station, retrace route to Kapitän-Alexander-Strasse in Cuxhaven. Turn L at traffic lights (Konrad-Adenauer-Allee) then first L into station car park. ◄

*Regular trains run from Cuxhaven to Hamburg and Bremerhaven.*

# APPENDIX A

*Facilities summary*

| | Distance (km) | Cumulative distance (km) | Altitude (m) | Accommodation | Youth hostel | Food | Camping | Tourist office | Cycle shop | Station |
|---|---|---|---|---|---|---|---|---|---|---|
| **Prologue** | | | | | | | | | | |
| Vrchlabí station | 0 | 0 | 467 | x | | x | x | x | x | x |
| Hořejší Vrchlabí | 4 | 4 | 516 | x | | x | | | | |
| Herlikovice | 2 | 6 | 564 | x | | x | | | | |
| Labská dam | 7.5 | 13.5 | 699 | x | | | | | | |
| Špindlerův Mlýn | 2.5 | 16 | 722 | x | | x | x | x | | |
| Medvědín | 3 | 19 | 1233 | | | x | | | | |
| Vrbatova bouda | 4.5 | 23.5 | 1390 | | | x | | | | |
| Labská bouda | 3 | 26.5 | 1340 | x | | x | | | | |
| **Stage 1** | | | | | | | | | | |
| Labská bouda | 0 | 0 | 1340 | x | | x | | | | |
| Vrbatova bouda | 3 | 3 | 1390 | | | x | | | | |
| Horní Mísečky | 5 | 8 | 1036 | x | | x | | | | |
| Rovinka | 6.5 | 14.5 | 853 | | | x | | | | |
| Benecko | 3.5 | 18 | 866 | x | | x | | | | |
| Vrchlabí station | 6.5 | 24.5 | 486 | x | | x | x | x | x | x |
| Podhůří | 4 | 28.5 | 438 | | | | | | | x |
| Kunčice n/L | 2.5 | 31 | 413 | | | | | | | x |
| Klášterská Lhota | 4 | 35 | 379 | | | | | | | x |
| Prosečné | 3 | 38 | 362 | | | | | | | x |
| Hostinné | 2 | 40 | 352 | x | | x | | x | | x |
| **Stage 2** | | | | | | | | | | |
| Horní Debrné | 7 | 47 | 332 | x | | | | | | |
| Nemojov | 4.5 | 51.5 | 404 | x | | x | | | | |
| Les Královstvi dam | 2 | 53.5 | 330 | | | x | | | | |
| Dvůr Králové n/L | 6 | 59.5 | 288 | x | | x | x | x | x | x |
| Žireč | 5 | 64.5 | 279 | | | x | | | | x |

| | Distance (km) | Cumulative distance (km) | Altitude (m) | Accommodation | Youth hostel | Food | Camping | Tourist office | Cycle shop | Station |
|---|---|---|---|---|---|---|---|---|---|---|
| Stanovice | 2 | 66.5 | 273 | x | | x | | | | |
| Kuks | 1.5 | 68 | 268 | x | | x | | x | | x |
| Brod | 2.5 | 70.5 | 263 | | | x | | | | |
| Heřmanice | 1.5 | 72 | 262 | | | x | | | | |
| Jaroměř | 3.5 | 75.5 | 252 | x | | x | | x | | x |
| **Stage 3** | | | | | | | | | | |
| Josefov | 2 | 77.5 | 253 | x | | x | | | | |
| Cernožice | 4.5 | 82 | 250 | | | x | | | | x |
| Smiřice | 2.5 | 84.5 | 243 | | | x | | | | x |
| Lochenice | 6 | 90.5 | 239 | | | x | | | | x |
| Předměřice n/L | 2 | 92.5 | 239 | | | x | | | | x |
| Plácky | 3.5 | 96 | 233 | | | x | | | | |
| Hradec Králové | 2 | 98 | 233 | x | | x | | x | x | x |
| Moravské Předměstí | 3 | 101 | 230 | x | | x | | | | |
| Vysoká n/L | 6 | 107 | 234 | x | | x | | | | |
| Dříteč | 6 | 113 | 226 | | | x | | | | |
| Kunětická Hora | 2.5 | 115.5 | 234 | x | | x | | x | | |
| Ráby | 3.5 | 116.5 | 220 | | | x | | x | x | |
| Brozany | 1 | 117.5 | 220 | | | x | | | | |
| Pardubice | 4 | 121.5 | 220 | x | | x | x | x | x | x |
| **Stage 4** | | | | | | | | | | |
| Svitkov | 4.5 | 126 | 217 | x | | | | | | x |
| Opočínek | 7 | 133 | 218 | | | | | | | x |
| Valy | 3 | 136 | 216 | | | x | | | | x |
| Mělice | 0.5 | 136.5 | 215 | | | x | x | | | |
| Lohenice | 2 | 138.5 | 213 | | | x | | | | |
| Břehy | 2.5 | 141 | 213 | | | x | x | x | | |
| Semín | 5 | 146 | 211 | | | x | x | | | |
| Kladruby n/L | 2.5 | 148.5 | 209 | | | x | | | | |
| Selmice | 4 | 152.5 | 204 | | | x | | | | |
| Týnec n/L | 7 | 159.5 | 237 | x | | x | x | x | | x |

| | Distance (km) | Cumulative distance (km) | Altitude (m) | Accommodation | Youth hostel | Food | Camping | Tourist office | Cycle shop | Station |
|---|---|---|---|---|---|---|---|---|---|---|
| Lžovice | 2.5 | 162 | 238 | | | x | | | | |
| Kolín | 11.5 | 173.5 | 197 | x | | x | | x | x | x |
| **Stage 5** | | | | | | | | | | |
| Velký Osek | 10.5 | 184 | 194 | x | | x | | | | x |
| Libice n/C | 3.5 | 187.5 | 189 | | | x | | | | x |
| Poděbrady | 5 | 192.5 | 188 | x | | x | | x | x | x |
| Velké Zboži | 3 | 195.5 | 185 | | | x | | | | x |
| Nymburk | 5.5 | 201 | 189 | x | | x | | x | x | x |
| **Stage 6** | | | | | | | | | | |
| Drahelice | 2.5 | 203.5 | 185 | | | x | | | | |
| Ostrá | 11.5 | 215 | 178 | | | x | x | | | |
| Čelákovice | 13 | 228 | 171 | x | | x | | x | x | x |
| Lázně Toušeň | 4.5 | 232.5 | 171 | | | x | | | | x |
| Zeleneč | 5.5 | 238 | 256 | | | x | | | | x |
| Horni Počernice | 4.5 | 242.5 | 285 | x | | x | | | | x |
| Černý Most | 2.5 | 245 | 254 | x | | x | | | | |
| Lehovec | 2.5 | 247.5 | 245 | | | | | | x | |
| Hloubětín | 0.5 | 248 | 219 | x | | x | | | | |
| Vysočany | 4.5 | 252.5 | 195 | x | | | | | x | x |
| Libeň | 3 | 255.5 | 185 | x | | | | | x | |
| *Prague (5km off route)* | *5* | *260.5* | *191* | x | x | x | | x | x | x |
| **Stage 7** | | | | | | | | | | |
| Troja | 4.5 | 260 | 182 | x | | x | x | | | |
| Zámky | 3.5 | 263.5 | 184 | | | x | | | | |
| Klecany | 4.5 | 268 | 247 | | | x | | | x | |
| Dol ferry | 7.5 | 275.5 | 176 | | | x | | | | |
| Chvatěruby | 3.5 | 279 | 171 | | | x | | | | x |
| Lobeček | 2.5 | 281.5 | 176 | | | | | | | |
| Kralupy n/V | 1 | 282.5 | 174 | x | | x | | x | x | x |
| Nelahozeves | 2.5 | 285 | 174 | x | | x | | | | x |
| Miřejovice | 2 | 287 | 172 | x | | | x | | | |

| | Distance (km) | Cumulative distance (km) | Altitude (m) | Accommodation | Youth hostel | Food | Camping | Tourist office | Cycle shop | Station |
|---|---|---|---|---|---|---|---|---|---|---|
| Veltrusy palace | 1.5 | 288.5 | 172 | | | x | | | | |
| Dušníky n/V | 4.5 | 293 | 167 | x | | x | | | | |
| Dědibaby | 1.5 | 294.5 | 166 | | | x | | | | |
| Bukol | 2.5 | 297 | 169 | | | x | | | | |
| Lužec n/V | 1 | 298 | 160 | | | | | | | x |
| Hořín | 8.5 | 306.5 | 163 | | | x | | | | |
| Mělník bridge | 1 | 307.5 | 164 | x | | x | x | x | x | x |
| **Stage 7A** | | | | | | | | | | |
| *Brandýs n/L* | *3.5* | *3.5* | *174* | *x* | | | | *x* | *x* | *x* |
| *Záryby* | *5.5* | *9* | *167* | | | *x* | | | | |
| *Kostelec n/L* | *3* | *12* | *169* | | | | | | *x* | *x* |
| *Kly* | *13.5* | *25.5* | *163* | | | *x* | | | | |
| *Mělník* | *6.5* | *32* | *214* | *x* | | *x* | *x* | *x* | *x* | *x* |
| *Mělník bridge* | *1.5* | *33.5* | *164* | | | | | | | |
| **Stage 8** | | | | | | | | | | |
| Vliněves | 3 | 310.5 | 161 | | | x | | | | |
| Dolní Beřkovice | 2 | 312.5 | 161 | | | x | | | | x |
| Horni Počaply | 6.5 | 319 | 155 | x | | x | | | | x |
| Hnévice | 3 | 322 | 156 | | | | | | | x |
| Račice | 2 | 324 | 160 | x | | x | | | | |
| Záluží | 3 | 327 | 159 | | | | | | | x |
| Dobříň | 3.5 | 330.5 | 153 | x | | | | | | x |
| Roudnice n/L | 2.5 | 333 | 152 | x | | x | | x | x | x |
| Hrobce | 5.5 | 338.5 | 154 | | | x | | | | x |
| Libotenice | 2 | 340.5 | 155 | | | x | | | | |
| Terezín | 10.5 | 351 | 152 | x | | x | x | x | x | |
| Litoměřice | 3.5 | 354.5 | 152 | x | x | x | x | x | x | x |
| **Stage 9** | | | | | | | | | | |
| Žalhostice | 3.5 | 358 | 148 | | | x | | | | x |
| Píšťany | 1 | 359 | 148 | x | | x | | | | |
| Velké Žernoseky | 2.5 | 361.5 | 145 | x | | x | | | | x |

| | Distance (km) | Cumulative distance (km) | Altitude (m) | Accommodation | Youth hostel | Food | Camping | Tourist office | Cycle shop | Station |
|---|---|---|---|---|---|---|---|---|---|---|
| Libochovany | 4 | 365.5 | 151 | | | x | | | | x |
| Sebuzin | 5.5 | 371 | 152 | | | x | | | x | x |
| Brná n/L | 3 | 374 | 144 | x | | x | x | | | |
| Střekov dam | 3 | 377 | 145 | | | x | | | | x |
| *Ústí n/L (1km off route)* | *2.5* | *379.5* | *138* | *x* | | *x* | | *x* | *x* | *x* |
| Svádov | 4 | 383.5 | 134 | x | | | | | | x |
| Valtířov | 2 | 385.5 | 142 | | | x | | | | x |
| Velké Brezno | 2 | 387.5 | 136 | | | x | | | | x |
| Malé Březno | 2.5 | 390 | 135 | | | | | | | x |
| Těchlovice | 3.5 | 393.5 | 132 | | | | | | | x |
| Boltice n/L | 5.5 | 399 | 130 | | | | | | | x |
| Děčín | 6 | 405 | 130 | x | x | x | x | x | x | x |
| **Stage 10** | | | | | | | | | | |
| Připeř | 1 | 406 | 130 | | | | | | | x |
| Čertova Voda | 4.5 | 410.5 | 124 | | | | | | | x |
| Dolní Žleb | 3 | 413.5 | 125 | | | x | | | | x |
| Schöna | 4 | 417.5 | 124 | | | | | | | x |
| Hirschmühle ferry | 2 | 419.5 | 124 | | | | | | | x |
| Krippen | 5 | 424.5 | 121 | x | | x | | | | x |
| Postelwitz | 0.5 | 425 | 121 | x | | | | | x | |
| Bad Schandau | 1 | 426 | 120 | x | x | x | | x | x | x |
| **Stage 11** | | | | | | | | | | |
| Elbe Freizeitland | 5.5 | 431.5 | 124 | | | | x | | | |
| Königstein | 2 | 433.5 | 119 | x | | x | x | x | x | x |
| Thürmsdorf | 1.5 | 435 | 119 | x | | x | | | | |
| Oberrrathen | 4.5 | 439.5 | 121 | x | | x | | | | x |
| Pötzscha | 3 | 442.5 | 125 | x | | x | | | | x |
| Obervogelgesang | 3.5 | 446 | 114 | | | x | | | | x |
| Pirna | 4 | 450 | 113 | x | x | x | x | x | x | x |
| Heidenau | 4 | 454 | 116 | x | | x | | | x | x |

| | Distance (km) | Cumulative distance (km) | Altitude (m) | Accommodation | Youth hostel | Food | Camping | Tourist office | Cycle shop | Station |
|---|---|---|---|---|---|---|---|---|---|---|
| Zschieren | 3.5 | 457.5 | 112 | x | | x | | | | |
| Kleinschachwitz | 2 | 459.5 | 115 | x | | x | x | | | |
| Laubegast | 2 | 461.5 | 117 | x | | x | | | | |
| Blasewitz | 4.5 | 466 | 111 | x | | x | | | | |
| Dresden | 6 | 472 | 108 | x | x | x | | x | x | x |
| **Stage 12** | | | | | | | | | | |
| Gohlis | 9 | 481 | 107 | x | | | | | | |
| Niederwartha | 3.5 | 484.5 | 106 | | | x | | | | x |
| Wildberg | 2 | 486.5 | 108 | x | | x | | | | |
| Constappel | 1.5 | 488 | 106 | x | | x | | | | |
| Reppina | 3.5 | 491.5 | 103 | x | | x | | | | |
| Rehbocktal | 3 | 494.5 | 103 | | | x | x | | | |
| Siebeneichen | 1.5 | 496 | 103 | | | x | | | | |
| Meissen | 1.5 | 497.5 | 101 | x | | x | | x | x | x |
| **Stage 13** | | | | | | | | | | |
| Keilbusch | 3.5 | 501 | 103 | | | x | | | | |
| Zehren | 3.5 | 504.5 | 102 | x | | | | | | |
| Hebelei | 4.5 | 509 | 108 | x | | | | | | |
| Niederlommatzsch | 0.5 | 509.5 | 98 | x | | x | | | | |
| Neuhirschstein | 1.5 | 511 | 98 | | | x | | | | |
| Boritz | 2.5 | 513.5 | 98 | | | x | | | | |
| Schänitz | 1.5 | 515 | 102 | | | | | | x | |
| Riesa | 8 | 523 | 108 | x | | x | x | x | x | x |
| **Stage 14** | | | | | | | | | | |
| Oppitzsch | 6 | 529 | 94 | x | | x | | | | |
| Strehla | 2.5 | 531.5 | 94 | x | x | x | x | | x | |
| Nixstein | 1.5 | 533 | 94 | | | x | x | | | |
| Görzig | 1 | 534 | 94 | x | | x | | | | |
| Aussig | 8.5 | 542.5 | 91 | x | | | | | | |
| *Mühlberg* (3km off route) | 8.5 | 548 | 89 | x | | x | | x | x | |

| | Distance (km) | Cumulative distance (km) | Altitude (m) | Accommodation | Youth hostel | Food | Camping | Tourist office | Cycle shop | Station |
|---|---|---|---|---|---|---|---|---|---|---|
| Belgern | 9 | 557 | 85 | x | | x | x | | x | |
| Wessnig | 8.5 | 565.5 | 88 | | | x | | | | |
| Bennewitz | 1.5 | 567 | 92 | | | x | | | | |
| Torgau | 6 | 573 | 84 | x | | x | | x | x | x |
| **Stage 15** | | | | | | | | | | |
| Döbern | 7 | 580 | 78 | x | | | | | | |
| Drebligar | 10 | 590 | 85 | | | x | | | | |
| Dommitzsch | 4 | 594 | 89 | x | | x | x | x | x | |
| Lausiger Teich | 8.5 | 602.5 | 87 | | | x | x | | | |
| Priesitz | 3 | 605.5 | 82 | x | | | | | | |
| Pretzsch ferry | 2.5 | 608 | 74 | x | | x | | | | x |
| Klöden | 7 | 615 | 76 | x | | x | x | | | |
| Schützberg | 3.5 | 618.5 | 72 | x | x | | | | | |
| Listerfehrda | 6 | 624.5 | 72 | x | | | | | | |
| Elster | 2 | 626.5 | 72 | x | | x | x | | x | x |
| Gallin | 6 | 632.5 | 71 | x | | x | | | | |
| Prühlitz | 1.5 | 634 | 72 | x | | | | | | x |
| Elstervorstadt | 4.5 | 638.5 | 71 | | | x | | | x | |
| Wittenberg | 3 | 641.5 | 74 | x | x | x | | x | x | x |
| **Stage 16** | | | | | | | | | | |
| Kleinwittenberg | 3 | 644.5 | 69 | | | | | | x | x |
| Piesteritz | 2 | 646.5 | 72 | x | | x | | | x | x |
| Griebo | 6.5 | 653 | 73 | | | x | | | | x |
| Coswig | 4.5 | 657.5 | 65 | x | | x | | x | | x |
| Coswig ferry | 1 | 658.5 | 62 | x | | x | | | | |
| Wörlitz | 4.5 | 663 | 61 | x | | x | | x | x | x |
| Vockerode | 4.5 | 667.5 | 65 | x | | x | | | | |
| Forsthaus | 6 | 673.5 | 62 | x | | x | | | | |
| Waldersee | 3 | 676.5 | 60 | x | | x | | | | x |
| Dessau | 4 | 680.5 | 60 | x | x | x | | x | x | x |

| | Distance (km) | Cumulative distance (km) | Altitude (m) | Accommodation | Youth hostel | Food | Camping | Tourist office | Cycle shop | Station |
|---|---|---|---|---|---|---|---|---|---|---|
| **Stage 17** | | | | | | | | | | |
| Kornhaus | 4.5 | 685 | 60 | | | x | x | | | |
| Grosskühnau | 3.5 | 688.5 | 59 | x | | x | | | | |
| Aken | 9.5 | 698 | 55 | x | | x | x | | x | |
| Steutz | 3.5 | 701.5 | 66 | x | | x | | | | |
| Steckby | 4 | 705.5 | 61 | x | | x | | | | |
| Walternienburg | 12 | 717.5 | 55 | x | | x | | | | |
| Ronney | 2.5 | 720 | 49 | x | | x | | | | |
| Barby | 2 | 722 | 54 | x | | x | | | | |
| **Stage 18** | | | | | | | | | | |
| Pömmelte | 7 | 729 | 52 | x | | x | | | | |
| Glimde | 2.5 | 731.5 | 49 | x | | x | | | | |
| Schönebeck | 10.5 | 742 | 50 | x | | x | | x | x | x |
| Frohse | 2.5 | 744.5 | 48 | x | | | x | | | x |
| Westerhüsen | 5 | 749.5 | 55 | | | x | | | | |
| Salbke | 1 | 750.5 | 52 | | | x | | | | x |
| Buckau | 6 | 756.5 | 48 | | | x | | | | x |
| Magdeburg | 2 | 758.5 | 45 | x | x | x | | x | x | x |
| **Stage 19** | | | | | | | | | | |
| Bruckfeld | 3 | 761.5 | 48 | | | x | | | | |
| Herrenkrug | 1.5 | 763 | 45 | x | | x | | | | x |
| Alt Lostau | 9.5 | 772.5 | 41 | x | | x | | | | |
| Hohenwarthe | 3.5 | 776 | 42 | x | | x | | | | |
| Niegripp | 7.5 | 783 | 42 | x | | x | x | | | |
| Schartau | 3.5 | 786.5 | 41 | x | | x | | | | |
| Rogätz | 3.5 | 790 | 43 | x | | x | | | | x |
| **Stage 20** | | | | | | | | | | |
| Bertingen | 8.5 | 798.5 | 45 | x | | x | x | | | |
| Kehnert | 1.5 | 800 | 44 | x | | x | | | | |
| Ringfurth | 6 | 806 | 45 | | | x | | | | |
| Bittkau | 6 | 812 | 41 | x | | x | x | | | |

| | Distance (km) | Cumulative distance (km) | Altitude (m) | Accommodation | Youth hostel | Food | Camping | Tourist office | Cycle shop | Station |
|---|---|---|---|---|---|---|---|---|---|---|
| Grieben | 3 | 815 | 40 | x | | x | | | | |
| Schelldorf | 4 | 819 | 35 | x | | | | | | |
| Buch | 3.5 | 822.5 | 35 | x | | x | | | | |
| Tangermünde | 7.5 | 830 | 45 | x | | x | x | x | x | x |
| **Stage 21** | | | | | | | | | | |
| Hamerten | 6 | 836 | 35 | | | | | | | x |
| Storkau | 3 | 839 | 39 | x | | x | | | | |
| Arneburg | 7 | 846 | 56 | x | | x | x | x | x | |
| Büttnersdorf | 13.5 | 859.5 | 28 | x | | x | x | | | |
| Sandau | 3 | 862.5 | 33 | x | | x | | | | |
| Havelberg | 4 | 866.5 | 29 | x | | x | x | x | x | |
| **Stage 21 Alternative** | | | | | | | | | | |
| *Nitzow* | *6.5* | *6.5* | *43* | *x* | | *x* | | | | |
| *Quitzöbel* | *6* | *12.5* | *27* | *x* | | *x* | | | | |
| *Abendorf* | *7.5* | *20* | *31* | | | *x* | | | | |
| **Stage 22** | | | | | | | | | | |
| Gnevsdorf | 19.5 | 886 | 25 | x | | | | | | |
| Bälow | 6 | 892 | 26 | x | | x | | | | |
| Hinzdorf | 4.5 | 896.5 | 28 | x | | x | | | | |
| Garsedow | 4 | 900.5 | 25 | x | | | x | | | |
| Wittenberge | 3 | 903.5 | 24 | x | | x | | x | x | x |
| **Stage 23** | | | | | | | | | | |
| Muggendorf | 10 | 913.5 | 24 | | | x | | | | |
| Cumlosen | 4.5 | 918 | 24 | x | | x | | | | |
| Lütkenwisch | 5.5 | 923.5 | 21 | x | | x | | | | |
| Lenzen ferry | 11 | 934.5 | 20 | | | x | | | | |
| Mödlich | 4 | 938.5 | 20 | x | | x | | | | |
| Unbesandten | 9.5 | 948 | 19 | x | | x | | | | |
| Dömitz | 8.5 | 956.5 | 20 | x | | x | x | x | x | |
| **Stage 24** | | | | | | | | | | |
| Kamerun | 6.5 | 963 | 16 | x | | | | | | |

| | Distance (km) | Cumulative distance (km) | Altitude (m) | Accommodation | Youth hostel | Food | Camping | Tourist office | Cycle shop | Station |
|---|---|---|---|---|---|---|---|---|---|---|
| Damnatz | 1.5 | 964.5 | 17 | x | | x | | | | |
| Wussegel | 10.5 | 975 | 14 | | | x | | | | |
| Hitzacker | 3 | 978 | 14 | x | x | x | | x | x | x |
| Tiessau | 6 | 984 | 18 | x | | x | x | | | |
| Drethem | 5 | 989 | 18 | x | | x | x | | | |
| Klein Kühren | 4 | 993 | 18 | | | x | x | | | |
| Neu Darchau | 2 | 995 | 14 | | | | | | | |
| Katemin | 0.5 | 995.5 | 16 | x | | | | | | |
| Walmsburg | 2.5 | 998 | 15 | | | x | | | | |
| Alt Garge | 4.5 | 1002.5 | 15 | x | | x | | | | |
| Bleckede | 7.5 | 1010 | 12 | x | | x | | x | x | x |
| **Stage 25** | | | | | | | | | | |
| Radegast | 7.5 | 1017.5 | 11 | | | x | x | | | |
| Brackede | 2 | 1019.5 | 13 | | | x | | | | |
| Grünendeich | 4 | 1023.5 | 7 | | | | x | | | |
| Sassendorf | 6.5 | 1030 | 10 | x | | x | x | | | |
| Hohnstorf | 1.5 | 1031.5 | 7 | | | x | x | | | |
| Lauenburg | 1.5 | 1033 | 11 | x | x | x | | x | x | x |
| Glüsing | 9 | 1042 | 20 | x | | x | | | | |
| Tesperhude | 2 | 1044 | 11 | x | | x | | | | |
| Krümmel | 1.5 | 1045.5 | 8 | x | | x | | | | x |
| Geesthacht | 4.5 | 1050 | 9 | x | x | x | | x | x | x |
| **Stage 26** | | | | | | | | | | |
| Altengamme | 7.5 | 1057.5 | 7 | x | | x | | | | |
| Riepenburger windmill | 6.5 | 1064 | 5 | | | x | | | | |
| Teufelsort | 1.5 | 1065.5 | 4 | | | x | | | | |
| Fünfhausen | 5.5 | 1071 | 4 | | | x | | | | |
| Ochsenwerder | 5 | 1076 | 4 | x | | x | | | | |
| Tatenberg | 2.5 | 1078.5 | 7 | x | | x | | | | |
| Rothenburgsort | 5 | 1083.5 | 8 | x | | x | | | | x |
| Hamburg | 6 | 1089.5 | 6 | x | x | x | | x | x | x |

| | Distance (km) | Cumulative distance (km) | Altitude (m) | Accommodation | Youth hostel | Food | Camping | Tourist office | Cycle shop | Station |
|---|---|---|---|---|---|---|---|---|---|---|
| **Stage 27** | | | | | | | | | | |
| Finkenwerder | 7 | 1096.5 | 0 | x | | x | | | x | |
| Neuenfelde | 10 | 1106.5 | 4 | x | | x | | | | |
| Cranz schleuse | 1 | 1107.5 | 6 | x | | x | | | | |
| Borstel | 8 | 1115.5 | 2 | x | | x | | | x | |
| Neuenschleuse | 2 | 1117.5 | 2 | x | | x | | | | |
| Wisch | 2 | 1119.5 | 2 | x | | x | | | | |
| Lühe | 1.5 | 1121 | 2 | x | | x | | | | |
| Grünendeich | 2.5 | 1123 | 3 | x | | x | | | x | |
| Twielenfleth | 4 | 1127.5 | 8 | | | x | | | x | |
| Stade | 7 | 1134.5 | 6 | x | x | x | | x | x | x |
| **Stage 28** | | | | | | | | | | |
| Schölish | 1 | 1135.5 | 1 | x | | x | | | | |
| Bützfleth | 5 | 1140.5 | 2 | x | | | | | | |
| Krautsand | 15 | 1155.5 | 4 | x | | x | x | | x | |
| Dornbusch | 3.5 | 1159 | 5 | | | x | | | x | |
| Neulandermoor | 5 | 1164 | 2 | x | | x | | | | |
| Wischhafen | 4 | 1168 | 3 | x | | x | | x | x | |
| Freiburg | 8 | 1176 | 7 | x | | x | | | | |
| **Stage 29** | | | | | | | | | | |
| Hörne | 20.5 | 1196.5 | 4 | x | | x | | | | |
| Belum | 9 | 1205.5 | 4 | | | | | | x | |
| Otterndorf schleuse | 6.5 | 1212 | 8 | x | x | x | | x | x | x |
| Achtern Diek | 2 | 1214 | 2 | | | x | x | | | |
| Altenbruch schleuse | 7.5 | 1221.5 | 6 | x | | x | x | | | |
| Cuxhaven | 6 | 1227.5 | 2 | x | x | x | x | x | x | x |

# APPENDIX B
*Tourist information offices*

**Stage 1**
Špindlerův Mlýn
Svatopetrská 173
53451
tel +420 499 523 656
www.mestospindleruvmlyn.cz

Vrchlabí
Krknošská 8
54301
tel +420 499 405 744
www.muvrchlabi.cz

Hostinné
Náměstí 69
54371
tel +420 499 404 746
www.hostinne.info

**Stage 2**
Dvůr Králové nad Labem
nám T G Masaryka 2
54417
tel +420 499 321 742
www.dvurkralove.cz

Kuks
Kuks 12
54443
tel +420 499 422 423
www.zkuskuks.cz

Jaroměř
nám Československé armády 16
55101
tel +420 491 847 220
www.jaromer-josefov.cz

**Stage 3**
Hradec Králové
Velké nám 166/1
50001
tel +420 495 580 492
www.ic-hk.cz

Ráby
V Perníkové chaloupka čp38
53352
tel +420 466 612 474
www.pernikova-chaloupka.cz

Pardubice
nám Republiky 1
53002
tel +420 775 068 390
www.ipardubice.cz

**Stage 4**
Přelouč
Masarykovo nám 26
53501
tel +420 466 672 259
www.kicmp.cz

Týnec nad Labem
Komenského nám 235
28126
tel +420 321 781 505
www.tictynec.cz

Kolín
Brandlova 35
28002
tel +420 311 510 866
www.tickolin.cz

**Stage 5**
Poděbrady
Jiřiho nám 19
29001
tel +420 325 511 946
www.polabi.com

Nymburk
nám Přemyslovců 165/1
828828
tel +420 325 501 104
www.mesto-nymburk.cz

**Stage 6**
Lysá nad Labem
Husovo nám 23/1
28922
tel +420 601 323 046
www.pruhpolabi.cz

Čelákovice
Městské museum
Na Hrádku 464
25088
tel +420 315 558 937
www.celmuz.cz

Prague (Old Town Hall)
Staroměstské nám 1
11000 Praha 1 Staré Město
tel +420 221 714 444
www.prague.eu

**Stage 7**
Kralupy nad Vltavou
Palackého nám 1
27801
tel +420 315 739 811
www.infokralupy.cz

Mělník
Legionářů 51
27601
tel +420 315 627 503
www.ticmelnik.cz

**Stage 7A**
Brandýs nad Labem
Masarykovo nám 1
25001
tel +420 326 909 188
www.brandysko.cz

**Stage 8**
Roudnice nad Labem
Arnoštova 88
41301
tel +420 412 871 501
www.vyletnarip.cz

Terezín
Retranchement 5
Dukelských hrdinů 43
41155
tel +420 775 711 881
www.terezin.cz

Litoměřice
Mírové nám 16/8a
41201
tel +420 416 916 440
tel +420 416 732 440
www.litomerice.cz/infocentrum

**Stage 9**
Ústí nad Labem
Mírové nám 1/1
40001
tel +420 475 271 700
www.usti-nad-labem.cz

Děčín
K Čapka 1441/3
40655
tel +420 412 532 227
www.idecin.cz

**Stage 10**
Bad Schandau
Haus des Gastes
Marktplatz 12
01814
tel +49 3502 290030
www.bad-schandau.de

**Stage 11**
Königstein
Pirnaer Strasse 2
01824
tel +49 3502 168261
www.koenigstein-sachsen.de

Pirna
Am Markt 7
01796
tel +49 3501 556446
www.pirna.de

Dresden
Neumarkt 2
01607
tel +49 351 501501
www.dresden.de

## Stage 12
Meissen
Markt 3
01662
tel +49 352 141940
www.touristinfo-meissen.de

## Stage13
Riesa
Hauptstrasse 61
01589
tel +49 352 5529420
www.riesa.de

## Stage 14
Strehla
Am Schlosspark 1
01616
tel +49 352 6490739
www.strehla.de

Torgau
Markt 1
04860
tel +49 342 170140
www.tic-torgau.de

## Stage 15
Dommitzsch
Markt 3
04880
tel +49 342 2343924
www.dommitzsch.de

Wittenberg
Schlossplatz 2
06886
tel +49 349 1498610
www.lutherstadt-wittenberg.de

## Stage 16
Coswig
Am Markt 1
06869
tel +49 349 036100
www.coswigonline.de

Wörlitz
Förstergasse 26
06785
tel +49 349 0531009
www.woerlitz-information.de

Dessau
Zerbster Strasse 2c
06844
tel +49 340 2041442
www.visitdessau.com

## Stage 18
Schönebeck
Markt 21
39218
tel +49 392 8842742
www.solepark.de

Magdeburg
Breiter Weg 22
39104
tel +49 391 63601402
www.magdeburg-tourist.de

## Stage 20
Tangermünde
Markt 2
39590
tel +49 393 2222393
www.tourismus-tangermuende.de

## Stage 21
Arneburg
Breite Strasse 16
39596
tel +49 393 2151817
www.stadt-arneburg.de

Havelberg
Uferstrasse 1
39539
tel +49 393 8779091
www.havelberg.de

**Stage 22**
Wittenberge
Paul-Linke-Platz 1
19322
tel +49 387 7929181
www.wittenberge.de

**Stage 23**
Dömitz
Rathausplatz 1
19303
tel +49 387 5822112
www.doemitz.de

**Stage 24**
Hitzacker
Am Markt 7
29456
tel +49 586 296970
www.wendland-elbe.de

Bleckede
Biosphaerium Elbtalaue
Schlossstrasse 10
21354
tel +49 585 2951414
www.bleckede-tourismus.de

**Stage 25**
Lauenburg
Elbstrasse 59
21481
tel +49 415 35909220
www.herzogtum-lauenburg.de/lauenburg

Geesthacht
Krügerschen Haus
Bergedorfer Strasse 28
21502
tel +49 415 2836258
www.herzogtum-lauenburg.de/geesthacht

**Stage 26**
Hamburg
Hauptbahnhof Hamburg
Kirchenalee
20095
tel +49 403 0051701
www.hamburg-tourism.de

**Stage 27**
Stade
Hansestrasse 16
21682
tel +49 414 1776980
www.stade-tourismus.de

**Stage 28**
Wischhafen
Stader Strasse 175
21737
tel +49 477 0831129
www.tourismus-kehdingen.de

**Stage 29**
Otterndorf
Wallstrasse 12
21762
tel +49 475 1919131
www.otterndorf.de

Cuxhaven
Cuxhavener Strasse 92
27476
tel +49 472 1404200
www.nordseeheilbad-cuxhaven.de

# APPENDIX C
*Youth hostels*

**Stage 6**
Prague Downtown
Národní 19
11000 Praha 1 Staré Město
tel +420 224 240570
downtown@jsc.cz

Prague Advantage
Sokolská 11
12000 Praha 2 Nové Město
tel +420 224 914062
advantage@jsc.cz

Prague Pension Beta
Jaromírova 46/174
12800 Praha 2 Nusle
tel +420 222 564385
pensionbeta@pensionbeta.cz

**Stage 8**
Litoměřice U sv Štěpána (170 beds)
Komenského 4
41201 Litoměřice
tel +420 416 732077
hostel@inprincipio.cz

**Stage 9**
Děčín (24 beds)
Čsl Mládeže 195/21
40502 Děčín
tel +420 777 286963
info@hostel-decin.cz

**Stage 10**
Bad Schandau (Ostrau) (101 beds)
Dorfstrasse 14
01814 Bad Schandau
tel +49 350 2242408
badschandau@jugendherberge.de

**Stage 11**
Copitz (opposite Pirna) Nature/Arts Hostel
(166 beds)
Zum Wesenitzbogen 9
01796 Pirna
tel +49 3501 445601
pirna@jugendherberge.de

Dresden Rudi Arndt (71 beds)
Hübnerstrasse 11
01069 Dresden
tel +49 351 4710667
dresden.rudiarndt@jugendherberge.de

Dresden Jugendgästehaus (480 beds)
Maternistrasse 22
01067 Dresden
tel +49 351 492620
dresden@jugendherberge.de

**Stage 14**
Strehla Graslöwen (70 beds)
Torgauer Strasse 33
01616 Strehla
tel +49 352 6492030
strehla@jugendherberge.de

**Stage 15**
Wittenberg Schloss (153 beds)
Schlossstrasse 14/15
06886 Wittenberg
tel +49 349 1505205
wittenberg@jugendherberge.de

**Stage 16**
Dessau-Rosslau house I (159 beds)
Ebertallee 151
06846 Dessau-Rosslau
tel +49 340 619803
dessau@jugendherberge.de

Dessau-Rosslau house II self-service
(34 beds)
Waldkaterweg 11
06846 Dessau-Rosslau
tel +49 340 619803
dessau@jugendherberge.de

**Stage 18**
Magdeburg (248 beds)
Leiterstrasse 10
39104 Magdeburg
tel +49 391 5321010
magdeburg@jugendherberge.de

**Stage 24**
Hitzacker (167 beds)
An der Wolfsschlucht 2
29456 Hitzacker
tel +49 586 2244
hitzacker@jugendherberge.de

**Stage 25**
Lauenburg Zündholzfabrik (79 beds)
Elbstrasse 2
21481 Lauenburg/Elbe
tel +49 415 359888
lauenburg-zuendholzfabrik@
jugendherberge.de

Lauenburg (124 beds)
Am Sportplatz 7
21481 Lauenburg/Elbe
tel +49 415 32598
lauenburg@jugendherberge.de

Geesthacht (110 beds)
Berliner Strasse 117
21502 Geesthacht
tel +49 415 22356
geesthacht@jugendherberge.de

**Stage 26**
Hamburg Horner Rennbahn (423 beds)
Rennbahnstrasse 100
22111 Hamburg
tel +49 405 5701590
hamburg-horn@jugendherberge.de

Hamburg Auf dem Stintfang (358 beds)
Alfred-Wegener-Weg 5
20459 Hamburg
tel +49 405 5701590
stintfang@jugendherberge.de

**Stage 27**
Stade (139 beds)
Kehdinger Mühren 11
21682 Stade
tel +49 414 146368
stade@jugendherberge.de

**Stage 29**
Otterndorf (195 beds)
Schleusenstrasse 147
21762 Otterndorf
tel +49 475 13165
otterndorf@jugendherberge.de

Cuxhaven Duhnen (251 beds)
Schlensenweg 2
27476 Cuxhaven-Duhnen
tel +49 472 148552
cuxhaven@jugendherberge.de

# APPENDIX D
*Ferries, lifting bridges and chairlifts*

Only services used in this book are listed. The COVID pandemic may have brought about some alterations in services since this information was compiled, so please check timings locally.

**Prologue**
Špindlerův Mlýn-Medvědin chairlift
mid May–early Nov, 0800–1800,
half hourly. Actual operating dates depend
upon weather conditions. Winter, no
cycles carried.

**Stage 7**
Bukol–Lužec nad Vltavou passenger ferry
Mon 0600–1000 and 1200–1900
Tue–Fri 0600–1900Sat/Sun 0800–1900
operates on demand

**Stage 10**
Krippen–Postelwitz passenger ferry
Frequent departures (between 13 and 43
mins past the hour) Apr–Oct, Mon–Fri
0613–2243, Sat/Sun/holidays 0813–2243
Nov–Mar, Mon–Fri 0613–1843, Sat/Sun/
holidays 0813–1843

**Stage 15**
Pretzsch–Mauken vehicle ferry
Apr–Oct, Mon–Fri 0500–1900, Sat/Sun/
holidays 0800–1800
Nov–Mar, Mon–Fri 0500–1800, Sat/Sun/
holidays 0800–1600

**Stage 16**
Coswig–Wörlitz vehicle ferry
Mar and Nov, 1000–1700
Apr and Oct, 0900–1800
May–Sep, 0900–2100

**Stage 17**
Aken–Steutz vehicle ferry
All year, Mon–Fri 0530–2000
Apr–Sep, Sat 0700–2000, Sun 0800–2000
Oct–Mar, Sat 0800–1900, Sun 0900–1900

Ronney–Barby vehicle ferry
Apr–Oct, Mon–Fri 0515–2000, Sat/Sun/
holidays 0800–1900
Nov–Mar, Mon–Fri 0515–1830, Sat/Sun/
holidays 1000–1600

**Stage 19**
Schartau–Rogätz vehicle ferry
Apr–Sep, Mon–Fri 0545–2000, Sat/Sun
0800–2000
Oct–Mar, Mon–Fri 0600–1900, Sat/Sun
0900–1900
no crossing 1145–1230 (lunch break)

**Stage 21**
Büttnershof–Sandau vehicle ferry
Mar–Oct, Mon–Sat 0530–2130, Sun
0700–2130
Nov–Feb, Mon–Fri 0530–2000, Sat/Sun
0700–2000

**Stage 27**
Neumühlen/Övelgönne–Finkenwerder
riverbus Route 62
every 15mins 0515–2345

**Stage 28**
Wischhafen Süderelbe schleuse lifting
bridge
only open Sat/Sun and holidays May–
Sep,1000–1200 and 1700–1900
not passable at other times

**Stage 29**
Ostesperrwerk schleuse lifting bridge
open Tue–Thu all year 1000–1700;
Sat/Sun Apr–Sep 1000–1800, Oct–Mar
1000–1700
not passable Mon and Fri

# APPENDIX E
*Useful contacts*

**Transportation**
Eurostar
tel 0343 218 6186
(UK passenger reservations)
tel 0344 822 5822
(UK cycle reservations)
www.eurostar.com

Deutsche Bahn (German railways)
www.bahn.com

České dráhy (Czech railways)
www.cd.cz

NMBS/SNCB (Belgian railways)
www.belgiantrain.be

The Man in Seat 61 (rail travel information)
www.seat61.com

Wiggle (polythene bike bags)
www.wiggle.co.uk

Excess Baggage company
(airport bike boxes)
www.excess-baggage.com

**Cycling organisations**
Cycling UK (formerly CTC)
tel 01483 238301 (membership)
tel 0844 736 8458 (insurance)
www.cyclinguk.org

**Maps and guides**
Public Press (strip maps of route)
www.publicpress.de

Elbe Radweg official website
www.elbe-cycle-route.com

Open Street Maps (online mapping)
www.openstreetmap.org

Stanford's
7 Mercer Walk
London WC2H 9FA
tel 0207 836 1321
sales@stanfords.co.uk
www.stanfords.co.uk

The Map Shop
15 High St
Upton upon Severn, Worcs
WR8 0HJ
tel 01684 593146
themapshop@btinternet.com
www.themapshop.co.uk

**Accommodation**
Youth Hostels Association
(England & Wales)
tel 0800 0191700 or 01629 592700
www.yha.org.uk

SYHA (Scotland)
tel 01786 891400
www.hostellingscotland.org.uk

Jugendherberge
(German youth hostels)
www.jugendherberge.de

Hostelling International
(youth hostel bookings)
www.hihostels.com

Bett+bike
(German cycle-friendly accommodation)
www.bettundbike.de

# APPENDIX F
*Language glossary*

| English | German | Czech |
|---|---|---|
| please | *bitte* | *prosím* |
| thankyou | *danke(schön)* | *děkuji* |
| yes | *ja* | *ano* |
| no | *nein* | *ne* |
| beware | *Achtung* | *pozor* |
| bridge | *Brücke* | *most* |
| bicycle | *Fahrrad* | *kolo* |
| castle | *Schloss* | *hrad* |
| cathedral | *Dom* | *katedrála* |
| church | *Kirche* | *kostel* |
| cycle track | *Radweg* | *cyklostezka* |
| cyclist | *Radfahrer* | *cyklista* |
| dam | *Damm* | *přehrada* |
| diversion | *Umleitung* | *objížďka* |
| dyke | *Deich* | *hráz* |
| ferry | *Fähre* | *přívoz* |
| field | *Feld* | *pole* |
| floods | *Hochwasser* | *záplavy* |
| forest/woods | *Wald/Walder* | *les* |
| fort | *Festung* | *pevnost* |
| monastery | *Kloster* | *klášter* |
| monument | *Denkmal* | *památník* |
| motorway | *Autobahn* | *dálnice* |
| no entry | *Einfahrt verboten* | *zákaz vjezdu* |
| one way street | *Einbahnstrasse* | *jednosměrka* |
| puncture | *Reifenpanne* | *punkce* |
| railway | *(Eisen)bahn* | *železnice* |
| river | *Fluss* | *řeka* |
| riverbank | *Ufer* | *břeh řeky* |
| road closed | *Strasse gesperrt* | *silnice uzavřena* |
| station | *Bahnhof* | *nádraží/stanice* |
| tourist information office | *Fremdenverkehrsbüro* | *turistické informace* |
| town hall | *Rathaus* | *radnice* |
| youth hostel | *Jugendherberge* | *hostel mládeže* |

# DOWNLOAD THE ROUTES
# IN GPX FORMAT

All the routes in this guide are available for download from:

**www.cicerone.co.uk/1055/GPX**

as standard format GPX files. You should be able to load them into most online GPX systems and mobile devices, whether GPS or smartphone. You may need to convert the file into your preferred format using a conversion programme such as gpsvisualizer.com or one of the many other such websites and programmes.

When you follow this link, you will be asked for your email address and where you purchased the guidebook, and have the option to subscribe to the Cicerone e-newsletter.

www.cicerone.co.uk

# CICERONE

Trust Cicerone to guide your next adventure,
wherever it may be around the world...

Discover guides for hiking, mountain walking, backpacking,
trekking, trail running, cycling and mountain biking, ski touring,
climbing and scrambling in Britain, Europe and worldwide.

Connect with Cicerone online and find inspiration.

- buy books and ebooks
- articles, advice and trip reports
- podcasts and live events
- GPX files and updates
- regular newsletter

cicerone.co.uk